The Most Amazing Fact Book for Curious Kids

1200+ Fun and Interesting Facts from History, Science, Sports, Animals and More!

Trevor Fields

Table of Contents

CHAPTER 1:
Astonishing Universe

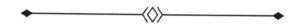

Fact 1: Even though the Sun seems close, it's actually about 93 million miles away from Earth. If you could drive there, going 60 mph, it would take 177 years!

Fact 2: A year on Mercury is just 88 Earth days. That means if you lived on Mercury, you'd have a birthday every three months!

Fact 3: Venus is the hottest planet in our solar system, even though Mercury is closer to the Sun. That's because Venus has a thick atmosphere that traps heat.

Fact 4: Mars is home to the tallest volcano we know of, Olympus Mons. It's about three times the height of Mount Everest, Earth's tallest mountain.

Fact 5: Jupiter has the biggest ocean of any planet, but it's not water, it's an ocean of hydrogen so deep that it turns into a metal!

Fact 6: Saturn isn't the only planet with rings, but its rings are the brightest and most massive. You could fit nearly one billion Earths across the length of all Saturn's rings!

Fact 7: Uranus rolls on its side as it orbits the Sun, which means it has really extreme seasons lasting 21 years each!

Fact 8: Neptune's winds are the fastest in the solar system, reaching speeds of 1,200 miles per hour. That's as fast as a commercial jet!

Fact 9: Pluto, now classified as a dwarf planet, has a heart-shaped glacier that's the size of Texas and Oklahoma combined.

Fact 10: The Milky Way, our galaxy, has about 100 billion stars, and it's just one of billions of galaxies in the universe.

Fact 11: If you could travel at the speed of light, you could go around the Earth 7.5 times in just one second.

Fact 12: Black holes are so strong they can pull in light, which is why we can't see them. They're like cosmic vacuum cleaners!

Fact 13: The largest known star, UY Scuti, is so big that if it were the Sun in our solar system, it would swallow everything up to Saturn.

Fact 14: Light from the Sun takes about 8 minutes and 20 seconds to reach Earth. So, the sunlight we see is actually a little bit old!

Fact 15: The first flower grown in space was a zinnia on the International Space Station. Imagine a space garden!

Fact 16: There are more trees on Earth than stars in the Milky Way galaxy, but there are more stars in the universe than grains of sand on all the Earth's beaches.

Fact 17: Space is completely silent because there's no air, which means sound can't travel through it. So, no one can hear you scream in space!

Fact 18: A day on Venus is longer than a year. It takes longer for Venus to spin on its axis once than it does for it to orbit the Sun.

Fact 19: The Moon is slowly moving away from Earth, about an inch and a half each year. Long ago, it was much closer to us.

Fact 20: There's a giant cloud of alcohol in outer space. It's too far away to bring to any parties, though, being 10,000 light-years away.

Fact 21: The deepest canyon in our solar system is on Mars. It's called Valles Marineris and is over 2,500 miles long and 7 miles deep.

Fact 22: One teaspoon of a neutron star would weigh about 6 billion tons because they are incredibly dense.

Fact 23: The first man-made object sent into space was in 1957 when the Soviet Union launched Sputnik, a small satellite.

Fact 24: Space is not completely empty; it's filled with tiny particles and bits of dust and gas, known as the interstellar medium.

CHAPTER 2:
Incredible Earth

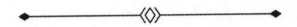

Fact 25: The deepest part of the ocean is called the Mariana Trench. It's so deep that if you put Mount Everest in it, the peak would still be underwater!

Fact 26: Earth has a super-powerful magnetic field, which is why compasses always point north. Without it, we'd be exposed to more solar radiation.

Fact 27: The Sahara Desert is the largest hot desert in the world, and it's almost as big as the United States!

Fact 28: Earth is the only planet we know of with liquid water on the surface. Thanks to our lakes, rivers, and oceans, Earth has the perfect recipe for life.

Fact 29: The Amazon Rainforest produces 20% of the world's oxygen. It's so big, it's like the lungs of our planet!

Fact 30: There are more than a thousand different kinds of bananas in the world, and they all grow in the tropics.

Fact 31: The Great Barrier Reef is the largest living structure on Earth. It's made up of thousands of tiny coral polyps and can be seen from space!

Fact 32: Earth's rotation is gradually slowing down. About a hundred years ago, a day was a millisecond shorter than today.

Fact 33: The Dead Sea is so salty that it's almost impossible to sink in it. You can easily float on the surface and read a book!

Fact 34: Mount Everest may be Earth's tallest mountain above sea level, but Mauna Kea, a volcano in Hawaii, is the tallest when measured from base to summit.

Fact 35: The Atacama Desert in Chile is so dry, some parts have never seen rain. It's like Mars on Earth!

Fact 36: Icebergs are huge chunks of ice that break off from glaciers. They can be as big as a country or as small as a piano.

Fact 37: The Nile River in Africa is the longest river in the world. It's so long; you could stack almost 30 Eiffel Towers along its length!

Fact 38: Earth's largest living organism isn't a whale or an elephant; it's a fungus! The Honey Fungus in Oregon covers 2.4 miles and is mostly underground.

Fact 39: Antarctica is the coldest place on Earth. It's so chilly, metal can break like glass, and your breath turns to snowflakes!

Fact 40: A bolt of lightning can be five times hotter than the surface of the sun. That's hotter than a pepperoni pizza oven!

Fact 41: Tornadoes can have wind speeds of over 300 mph. That's faster than race cars in the Indy 500!

Fact 42: The Angel Falls in Venezuela is the highest waterfall in the world. If you dropped a toy boat from the top, it would take 18 seconds to fall!

Fact 43: Earth's atmosphere stretches out to about 10,000 km, but 75% of it is within just 11 km of the surface. That's like having all the air squished into the bottom of a giant ocean of sky!

Fact 44: There's a river in Colombia called Caño Cristales that turns a rainbow of colors thanks to underwater plants. It's like Earth's own tie-dyed river!

Fact 45: The Pacific Ring of Fire is an area with a lot of earthquakes and volcanoes. It's where tectonic plates meet, which is like Earth doing a slow-motion bumper car game.

Fact 46: Alaska has over 3 million lakes. That's more lakes than all the rest of the US combined!

Fact 47: There's a place in Bolivia called Salar de Uyuni, which is the world's largest salt flat. When it rains, it becomes the world's largest mirror.

Fact 48: The Great Wall of China is so long that if you wanted to walk from one end to the other without stopping, it would take 18 months!

CHAPTER 3:
Prehistoric Life

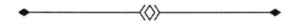

Fact 49: The Tyrannosaurus Rex had teeth up to 12 inches long, which is as big as a ruler. They used those giant teeth to chomp their dinner!

Fact 50: The Stegosaurus had a brain the size of a walnut, even though it was as big as a bus. That's one small brain for such a big dino!

Fact 51: Velociraptors were actually about the size of a turkey, not as big as the ones in the movies. They were still fast and fierce, though!

Fact 52: The Ankylosaurus had a tail like a club, and it could swing it hard enough to break the bones of its enemies. Talk about a knockout punch!

Fact 53: Dinosaurs lived on Earth for over 165 million years. That's about 825 times longer than humans have been around!

Fact 54: The Brontosaurus didn't chew its food. It swallowed stones that ground up the plants in its stomach!

Fact 55: Some dinosaurs had feathers, like the Sinosauropteryx, which had a fuzzy coat, even though it couldn't fly.

Fact 56: The smallest dinosaur egg ever found is about the size of a chicken egg. Maybe dinosaurs liked omelets too?

Fact 57: Pterosaurs were not dinosaurs but flying reptiles. The largest one had wings that were wider than a school bus is long!

Fact 58: The first dinosaur to be named was the Megalosaurus, back in 1824. That's nearly 200 years ago!

Fact 59: There were dinosaurs that lived in the water too, like the Elasmosaurus, which had a neck so long, it had more bones in its neck than a giraffe.

Fact 60: The Parasaurolophus had a long, hollow crest connected to its nose and could blast out sounds like a giant prehistoric trumpet.

Fact 61: The Argentinosaurus might have been the largest land animal ever, and its backbone was as big as a couch!

Fact 62: Many scientists believe that birds are the direct descendants of dinosaurs, which means dinosaurs are not completely extinct!

Fact 63: The Triceratops had three horns and a massive skull, making it one of the best-defended dinos in a headbutt contest.

Fact 64: Dinosaurs lived in every continent, even Antarctica. They were the global champions of hide and seek!

Fact 65: The Iguanodon, discovered in 1822, was one of the first dinosaurs ever found. It had spiky thumbs for protection.

Fact 66: The Spinosaurus is the largest carnivorous dinosaur discovered so far. It had a huge sail on its back and possibly swam in rivers.

Fact 67: Some prehistoric dragonflies had wingspans of over two feet. That's as wide as a baby's crib!

Fact 68: Before the dinosaurs, there were creatures called Trilobites that lived in the sea. They were one of the Earth's earliest known inhabitants.

Fact 69: The Woolly Mammoth was a prehistoric animal that lived at the same time as early humans. They had huge tusks and fur coats to keep them warm during the Ice Age.

Fact 70: There was a time called the Carboniferous Period when giant insects roamed the Earth, thanks to the high oxygen levels.

Fact 71: The Saber-Toothed Tiger, which wasn't really a tiger, had canines so long they were almost as big as a banana!

Fact 72: Cave bears lived alongside early humans, and they were enormous! Some were over 11 feet tall when standing on their hind legs.

CHAPTER 4:
Amazing Animals

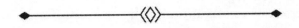

Fact 73: A group of flamingos is called a "flamboyance." They're pink because of the shrimp they eat, like a natural food dye for feathers!

Fact 74: The Pistol Shrimp can snap its claw so fast it creates a bubble hotter than the sun for a split second, and it makes a loud POP!

Fact 75: Sea otters hold hands when they sleep so they don't drift apart. They also use kelp as blankets to stay cozy.

Fact 76: The immortal jellyfish can actually reverse its aging process and start its life over. It's like hitting the ultimate redo button!

Fact 77: Hummingbirds can fly backwards and they have to eat at least half their body weight in sugar every day. That's like a kid eating 40 hamburgers!

Fact 78: Elephants have a special graveyard where they go when they feel they are going to die. They are like the wise elders of the animal kingdom.

Fact 79: Koalas have fingerprints that are so similar to humans', crime scene investigators can actually confuse the two!

Fact 80: A narwhal's long tusk is actually an overgrown tooth. Some refer to them as the unicorns of the sea because of their single, spiraled horn.

Fact 81: The mantis shrimp has one of the most powerful punches in nature, and they can see more colors than any other animal on Earth.

Fact 82: A group of crows is called a "murder," but there's nothing scary about them. They're actually very smart and can recognize human faces.

Fact 83: Parrotfish sleep in a bubble of their own mucus to hide their scent from predators. It's their own little slimy sleeping bag.

Fact 84: Sloths move so slowly that algae grow on their fur, giving them a greenish tint that acts as camouflage in the trees.

Fact 85: Giraffes have black tongues to prevent sunburn while they munch on leaves in the hot sun.

Fact 86: A cat's nose is as unique as a human's fingerprint. No two nose patterns are the same!

Fact 87: The axolotl can regenerate its body parts, including its heart and even parts of its brain. Talk about a superpower!

Fact 88: Frogs absorb water through their skin so they don't need to drink with their mouths. It's like having a built-in waterbed!

Fact 89: Honeybees can recognize human faces, which is pretty sweet for something with a brain the size of a sesame seed.

Fact 90: An octopus has three hearts and blue blood, and it can change both color and texture to blend into its surroundings.

Fact 91: Kangaroos can't walk backwards. It's like nature gave them an invisible bumper.

Fact 92: Some turtles can breathe through their butts, which is a handy trick for staying underwater longer.

Fact 93: The blue whale's heart is so big, a small child could swim through its arteries. That's a lot of heart!

Fact 94: The platypus is an odd animal that lays eggs, has a duck bill, webbed feet, and it's one of the few mammals that produce venom.

Fact 95: A group of jellyfish is called a "smack," and some jellyfish are as small as a pinhead while others have tentacles as long as a blue whale!

Fact 96: Ants can lift 10-50 times their body weight, which is like a kindergartner lifting a car. They're tiny but mighty!

CHAPTER 5:
Body Wonders

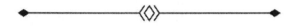

Fact 97: You have a unique tongue print, just like your fingerprints. No one else has a tongue pattern like yours!

Fact 98: Your nose can remember 50,000 different scents. It's like having a super-smell memory card inside your head!

Fact 99: Humans are the only animals that can blush. It's our body's way of showing we're embarrassed or excited.

Fact 100: When you take one step, you use up to 200 muscles. That's a lot of teamwork just to walk!

Fact 101: You grow new skin every 28 days. If you're around 10 years old, you've already shed about 100 layers of skin!

Fact 102: A human baby has 60 more bones than an adult. As you grow, some of those bones fuse together.

Fact 103: If you could unroll your brain, it would be about the size of a pillowcase. It's super wrinkly to fit inside your head!

Fact 104: The human eye can see millions of colors. It's like we all have our own personal rainbow detectors!

Fact 105: Your heart beats about 100,000 times in one day. That's like if you clapped your hands non-stop from breakfast till bedtime!

Fact 106: We lose about 40 to 100 strands of hair a day. But don't worry, you have about 100,000 strands on your head!

Fact 107: Your smallest bone is in your ear and it's called the stirrup bone, about the size of a rice grain.

Fact 108: You can't tickle yourself because your brain is too smart and it knows what you're up to!

Fact 109: Your body has about 5.6 liters (6 quarts) of blood; that would fill up about three big soda bottles.

Fact 110: Yawning helps cool down your brain when it gets too hot. It's like your brain's own air conditioner!

Fact 111: Your stomach gets a new lining every 2-3 days so that it doesn't digest itself with its own acid. Talk about self-protection!

Fact 112: The acid in your stomach is strong enough to dissolve zinc. It's like having a pool of super-powerful liquid inside you!

Fact 113: Every time you eat, your stomach has to rumble to mix up all the food like a shake machine.

Fact 114: You have two kidneys, but only one is necessary to live. They filter your blood and make pee.

Fact 115: Sneezes can shoot out of your nose at up to 100 miles per hour! That's faster than a car on the freeway!

Fact 116: The longest recorded hiccup attack lasted 68 years. Can you imagine hiccuping from kindergarten to being a grandparent?

Fact 117: Humans can make around 10,000 different facial expressions. It's like having an emoji board built into your face!

Fact 118: Your brain generates about 12-25 watts of electricity. This power could light up a low-wattage LED light bulb!

Fact 119: Right-handed people, on average, live longer than left-handed people. Don't worry lefties; it's only by a few years!

Fact 120: You can't breathe and swallow at the same time. Your body has a special switch to make sure you don't mix the two!

CHAPTER 6:
Inventive Genius

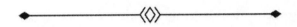

Fact 121: The first airplane wasn't comfy like today's planes. It was made of wood and paper and looked like a giant flying kite!

Fact 122: Bubble wrap was originally supposed to be wallpaper. Imagine having your walls pop every time you leaned on them!

Fact 123: The first computer was as big as a room and weighed as much as a small elephant. No one could have put it in their backpack!

Fact 124: Play-Doh wasn't always a plaything. It started as a wallpaper cleaner until someone realized it was more fun to make sculptures with it.

Fact 125: The slinky was invented by accident when an engineer was trying to make a spring to keep ships stable on rough seas. It ended up walking down stairs instead!

Fact 126: Potato chips were made by a chef who was annoyed with a customer who kept sending back his fried potatoes for being too thick. Talk about a tasty accident!

Fact 127: Popsicles were invented by an 11-year-old who left a mixture of powdered soda, water, and a stick in the cold overnight. That's one cool invention!

Fact 128: The man who invented the frisbee was turned into a frisbee after he died. He must have really loved flying in circles!

Fact 129: Band-Aids were created by a husband whose wife often cut herself while cooking. Now, we have a quick fix for our boo-boos!

Fact 130: Post-it Notes were the result of a failure. The glue was supposed to be super strong but ended up not sticking very well. Oops... or maybe not?

Fact 131: The microwave oven was invented after a scientist walked by a radar tube and the chocolate bar in his pocket melted. Talk about a hot discovery!

Fact 132: The first video game was made on a work computer, and it was a simple tennis game. It was more about fun than work!

Fact 133: Roller skates were first shown off at a fancy party in London. The inventor crashed into a huge mirror because he hadn't invented brakes yet!

Fact 134: The first vending machine was in ancient Egypt and gave out holy water. It wasn't for snacks or sodas!

Fact 135: The Ferris wheel was named after George Ferris, who built the first big one for the World's Fair in Chicago in 1893. It was like a giant bicycle wheel that could carry people!

Fact 136: The first digital camera was invented in 1975 and it took 23 seconds to take a photo. Say "slow cheese!"

Fact 137: The earliest alarm clock could only ring at 4 a.m. because it was made for workers. That's one early wake-up call!

Fact 138: The zipper was originally called a "clasp locker" when it was invented in 1893. It sounds like a wrestler's move!

Fact 139: The first pair of Nike shoes was made using a waffle iron for the sole pattern. It gave new meaning to "breakfast of champions!"

Fact 140: LEGO bricks were created by a carpenter from Denmark. They were wooden blocks originally and didn't click together like today's LEGOs.

Fact 141: Before erasers, people used bread crumbs to erase pencil marks. Imagine doing homework with a loaf of bread by your side!

Fact 142: The first sunglasses were used in China and were made from flat panels of smoky quartz. They were more about style than sun protection.

Fact 143: The first dishwasher was made by a woman who was tired of servants breaking her dishes. Necessity really is the mother of invention!

Fact 144: The first patented pencil with an eraser on top was in 1858. Before that, erasers and pencils were separate buddies!

CHAPTER 7:
Sealife

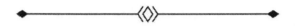

Fact 145: The ocean is home to the world's largest mountain range, the Mid-Oceanic Ridge. It's like a hidden spine for our planet, and it's all underwater!

Fact 146: The deepest part of the ocean is called the Mariana Trench. It's so deep that Mount Everest could fit inside it with room to spare!

Fact 147: Jellyfish have been around for more than 500 million years. That means they were cruising the oceans before dinosaurs were even a twinkle in Earth's eye!

Fact 148: Seahorses are tiny ocean riders, and guess what? The dads are the ones who carry the babies!

Fact 149: The Blue Whale, the largest animal on Earth, can have a heart as heavy as a car. Imagine the beep-beep of that heartbeat!

Fact 150: An octopus has three hearts and blue blood. Talk about an alien of the ocean!

Fact 151: Coral reefs are the bustling cities of the sea, but did you know they're alive? Corals are tiny animals, not plants.

Fact 152: There's a fish called the Parrotfish that sleeps in a bubble made of its own spit. It's like a gooey blanket for protection. Ew, but clever!

Fact 153: The ocean floor has lakes and rivers that flow with saltier water. It's a whole other world down there, with its own peaks and valleys.

Fact 154: A group of clownfish is called a school, but they don't need backpacks or lunchboxes!

Fact 155: Some starfish can regrow their arms if they lose one. And if the arm has a piece of the central body, it can grow an entirely new starfish!

Fact 156: The Pistol Shrimp can snap its claw so fast it creates a bubble hotter than the sun for a split second. That's some spicy seafood!

Fact 157: The Goblin Shark is called a 'living fossil' because it's so old in the terms of evolution. It's like a shark out of a storybook with a super pointy snout.

Fact 158: Lanternfish might not be famous, but they could be the most common fish in the ocean. They're like the secret stars of the sea.

Fact 159: Giant tube worms live near hydrothermal vents and can withstand crazy temperatures. They're like the superheroes of sea creatures.

Fact 160: The Mimic Octopus can change shape to look like other animals, like a sea snake or a flatfish. It's the master of sea disguises!

Fact 161: Some squids have a special skin that can change color and even create patterns. They're the groovy disco dancers of the ocean.

Fact 162: There's a type of algae that glows in the dark when the water moves. It's like the ocean's nightlight.

Fact 163: The Immortal Jellyfish can age backward, returning to a previous stage of its life. It's like it has a real-life time machine!

Fact 164: The Vampire Squid has a spooky name because it can turn its cape-like webbing inside out. Don't worry, it doesn't bite like a vampire!

Fact 165: The Peacock Mantis Shrimp has the most powerful punch in the ocean. It's like the heavyweight boxer of the sea!

Fact 166: Some male fish sing to attract females. It's their underwater love song.

Fact 167: Turtles can breathe through their rear ends. It sounds funny, but it's true!

Fact 168: The Maori Wrasse fish can change from female to male in its lifetime. It decides when it's time for a big change!

CHAPTER 8:
Flight and Exploration

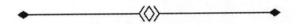

Fact 169: The Wright brothers made the first powered flight in 1903, but the flight only lasted 12 seconds. That's less time than it takes to tie your shoes!

Fact 170: Neil Armstrong's first step on the moon in 1969 was a big leap for mankind, but the footprint he left is still there today because there's no wind on the moon to blow it away.

Fact 171: Amelia Earhart was the first woman to fly solo across the Atlantic Ocean. She showed that the sky's the limit for everyone!

Fact 172: Space suits used by astronauts are super protective and can be really heavy. On Earth, they weigh up to 280 pounds—that's like carrying a refrigerator on your back!

Fact 173: The famous explorer Marco Polo traveled for 24 years before returning home. Imagine being on a road trip for that long!

Fact 174: Valentina Tereshkova, a Soviet cosmonaut, was the first woman to travel to space in 1963, orbiting Earth 48 times. Talk about going around in circles!

Fact 175: The Voyager 1 spacecraft is the furthest human-made object from Earth and has a golden record on board with sounds and pictures of Earth just in case it meets aliens!

Fact 176: Before there were airplanes, people would explore the world in hot air balloons. It was a slow ride with a great view!

Fact 177: The fastest jet aircraft ever, the SR-71 Blackbird, could fly faster than a speeding bullet. Superheroes, step aside!

Fact 178: Ferdinand Magellan's crew was the first to sail around the world, proving it was round and much bigger than anyone had thought.

Fact 179: The International Space Station zooms around Earth so fast that astronauts on board see 16 sunrises and sunsets each day. They have a lot of chances to get the perfect sunrise photo!

Fact 180: Sally Ride was the first American woman in space, and she used a special robotic arm to help satellites get where they needed to go.

Fact 181: The Montgolfier brothers invented the hot air balloon, and the first passengers were a sheep, a duck, and a rooster. What a wild barnyard ride!

Fact 182: The Webb Space Telescope, floating in space, takes such clear pictures of stars and galaxies that it's like having a super-powered camera.

Fact 183: Christopher Columbus sailed across the Atlantic hoping to find a new route to India, but instead, he stumbled upon the Americas.

Fact 184: The Space Shuttle could be used more than once to go to space, making it the world's first reusable spacecraft. It was like a space bus!

Fact 185: Roald Amundsen from Norway was the first explorer to reach the South Pole. It was so cold, he could have used a hot chocolate stand on the way!

Fact 186: The first living creatures to go to space and return safely were fruit flies. They went up in 1947 to see how space would affect living organisms.

Fact 187: Yuri Gagarin, the first man in space, had to parachute from his spaceship to land because it didn't have a safe way to touch down with him inside.

Fact 188: The Mars rovers are like remote-controlled cars, but instead of driving in your backyard, they're rolling across an entire planet.

Fact 189: In the early days of exploration, people thought the world was filled with mythical creatures like dragons and giant sea monsters. Imagine finding those in your local pond!

Fact 190: The Chinese explorer Zheng He commanded a huge fleet with ships so big, they were like floating palaces.

Fact 191: Bessie Coleman was the first African American woman to hold a pilot's license. She had to go to France to learn to fly because no one in the U.S. would teach her!

Fact 192: The New Horizons probe, which flew by Pluto, carries some of the ashes of the man who discovered the dwarf planet, Clyde Tombaugh. It's like he got to visit his discovery!

CHAPTER 9:
Microscopic Worlds

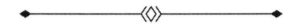

Fact 193: Your body has more bacteria cells than human cells.

Fact 194: Some bacteria are super helpful and make things like yogurt and cheese. They're like tiny chefs!

Fact 195: The world's smallest known bacteria is Mycoplasma genitalium, which is so tiny that 7,000 of them could fit inside a single red blood cell.

Fact 196: Viruses can't eat, breathe, or grow. They need to sneak into living cells to make more viruses, like a copy machine gone wild!

Fact 197: The common cold is caused by rhinoviruses, and "rhino" means "nose" in Greek – that's why your nose gets all stuffy!

Fact 198: Bacteria were some of the first life forms on Earth. They've been around for billions of years, way before dinosaurs.

Fact 199: Cells in your body are like tiny factories. They take in nutrients, make energy, and even send out waste.

Fact 200: There's a whole universe inside you! Your gut has good bacteria called probiotics that help digest your food.

Fact 201: Some bacteria can live in extreme places like hot springs, deep underground, or even in radioactive waste. They're the daredevils of the micro world!

Fact 202: Your saliva is full of bacteria-fighting compounds. It's like having a superhero in your mouth!

Fact 203: Bacteria can "talk" to each other using chemicals. It's their own secret language called quorum sensing.

Fact 204: Tardigrades, also known as water bears, are so tough they can survive in space. They're like the superheroes of the micro world!

Fact 205: The largest cell in the human body is the egg cell, and it's the only cell you can see without a microscope. It's like a speck of dust you can actually spot!

Fact 206: Viruses can sometimes mix with each other and swap parts. It's like they're doing a puzzle trade.

Fact 207: There are more microbes in a teaspoon of soil than there are people on Earth. It's a crowded underground city!

Fact 208: Red blood cells carry oxygen and make your blood look red. Without them, you'd be as pale as a ghost!

Fact 209: Bacteria in your mouth can create cavities, so brushing your teeth is like being a hero fighting tiny villains.

Fact 210: Some bacteria can 'eat' oil and are used to help clean up oil spills. They're like nature's cleaning crew!

Fact 211: Alexander Fleming discovered penicillin by accident when he noticed mold killing bacteria. Sometimes, messiness leads to greatness!

Fact 212: White blood cells in your body fight off bad germs. Think of them as your body's own team of superheroes.

Fact 213: The smallest virus is the Circovirus, and it's so tiny that 125,000 of them lined up end-to-end would be as wide as a human hair.

Fact 214: Some bacteria can form spores to survive harsh conditions, like a bear hibernating for a very, very long nap.

Fact 215: You have unique bacteria living on your skin, in your belly button, that's like having a fingerprint made of microbes!

Fact 216: Viruses can infect all sorts of living things, from plants and animals to bacteria. They're not picky about where they go to party!

CHAPTER 10:
Plant Kingdom

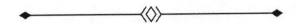

Fact 217: The Rafflesia arnoldii is known as the corpse flower because it smells like rotten meat. It uses this stinky scent to attract insects for pollination.

Fact 218: Bamboo can grow up to 91 cm (3 feet) in a single day. That's faster than you can climb up a slide!

Fact 219: Venus Flytraps capture bugs for a meal by snapping shut in less than a second. It's nature's own version of a bear trap!

Fact 220: The oldest living tree is a bristlecone pine named Methuselah, and it's over 4,800 years old. Imagine what stories it could tell if it could talk!

Fact 221: Sequoia trees can grow so tall that they tower over the Statue of Liberty. If trees could play basketball, they'd definitely win!

Fact 222: Some plants, like the sunflower, follow the sun across the sky in a motion called heliotropism. It's their daily sun-chasing dance.

Fact 223: Cacti can store water in their thick stems, which helps them survive in the desert. They're like natural water bottles!

Fact 224: The Amazon rainforest is so big that it produces 20% of the world's oxygen. It's often called the "lungs of the Earth."

Fact 225: There's a plant in Australia, the Gympie-Gympie, which has a sting so painful it can last for months. Best to admire this one from afar!

Fact 226: Orchids have the tiniest seeds in the world. It would take more than a million of them to weigh as much as a single paperclip.

Fact 227: The touch-me-not plant quickly closes its leaves when touched, which helps protect it from harm. It's a shy little thing.

Fact 228: A single oak tree can produce up to 10,000 acorns in one year. That's a lot of potential oak trees!

Fact 229: There are plants called epiphytes that live on the surface of other plants. They're not parasites; they just hang out and get their nutrients from the air and rain.

Fact 230: The giant water lily has leaves strong enough to hold a small child if the weight is evenly distributed. Still, it's not recommended as a raft!

Fact 231: Some plants can survive fires because their seeds need the heat to open and grow. Talk about rising from the ashes!

Fact 232: The cocoa tree produces the cocoa beans from which chocolate is made. It's a sweet treat that grows on trees!

Fact 233: There's a type of kelp, or seaweed, called Macrocystis that can grow up to 60 meters long. Underwater, it forms forests.

Fact 234: Plants don't just need sunlight to grow; they also need other plants around for healthy ecosystems. Diversity is key!

Fact 235: Pineapples grow as a result of numerous flowers whose individual berries merge together around a central core. It's a communal effort!

Fact 236: Pitcher plants lure insects into their "pitcher," filled with digestive liquid, where the insects drown and are digested. Nature's carnivorous cup!

Fact 237: The spice cinnamon comes from the bark of a tree. You could say it's tree-mendously tasty.

Fact 238: Mosses are among the oldest plants on earth, with some species unchanged for 400 million years. They're truly living fossils.

Fact 239: The Angel's Trumpet flower hangs down like a bell and can grow up to 50 cm (20 inches) long. It's a natural trumpet that's all beauty, no sound.

Fact 240: There are more than 60,000 tree species in the world, and each one plays a unique role in its ecosystem. Trees are the ultimate multitaskers!

CHAPTER 11:
Historical Highlights

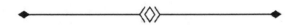

Fact 241: The Great Wall of China is so massive it took over 2,000 years to build. It's made of stone, brick, and hard work!

Fact 242: Ancient Egyptians slept on pillows made of stone. They believed it kept away bad spirits and also probably morning bedhead.

Fact 243: The wheel, invented over 5,500 years ago in Mesopotamia, wasn't used for transport at first, but as a potter's wheel to make pots.

Fact 244: The first Olympic Games in ancient Greece in 776 BC had only one event, a short sprint, and if you won, you were a hero for life.

Fact 245: Before alarm clocks, there were people called "knocker-ups" who tapped on windows with long sticks to wake people for work. Talk about a personal snooze button!

Fact 246: The first recorded flight of a hot air balloon was in 1783, and it carried a sheep, a duck, and a rooster. They were the first high-flying farm animals!

Fact 247: During the California Gold Rush in 1849, some people found gold without even looking for it, while others spent years and found nothing. It was like the world's biggest treasure hunt!

Fact 248: Cleopatra, the last pharaoh of Egypt, was known for her intelligence and could speak several languages.

Fact 249: The longest reigning monarch in history was Louis XIV of France, who stayed on the throne for 72 years and 110 days. That's a long time to wear a crown!

Fact 250: The first person to propose the idea of daylight saving time was Benjamin Franklin, but it wasn't taken seriously until many years later.

Fact 251: The first computer, called the ENIAC, was so big it filled an entire room and weighed as much as eight elephants.

Fact 252: The famous Leaning Tower of Pisa in Italy leans because its foundation was built on soft ground that couldn't support its weight. Oops!

Fact 253: The Aztec Empire was one of the first to have compulsory education for all children, regardless of gender or social status.

Fact 254: In medieval times, people believed that a king's touch could cure diseases. If only it were that easy!

Fact 255: The first pair of eyeglasses were invented in Italy around 1284. They've been helping people see the fine print ever since.

Fact 256: Julius Caesar's last words were not "Et tu, Brute?" as Shakespeare wrote, but historians are still unsure what he really said.

Fact 257: The Inca Empire built such durable roads and bridges in South America that some are still used today.

Fact 258: During the space race, astronauts aboard Apollo 11 left a mirror on the moon to measure the distance from Earth accurately.

Fact 259: Vikings were known for their longships, which were so well designed they could sail in deep ocean or shallow rivers.

Fact 260: In the early 1900s, horses were causing so much pollution with their waste that cars were seen as an environmentally friendly solution.

Fact 261: The ancient city of Pompeii was buried under volcanic ash in 79 AD and today provides a snapshot of Roman life frozen in time.

Fact 262: In the 1800s, some cities had wooden sidewalks and residents had to step down to the street, which is where the phrase "step down" comes from.

Fact 263: The Declaration of Independence was written on parchment, which is made from animal skin, because it's more durable than paper.

Fact 264: The famous explorer Marco Polo may have brought pasta back to Italy from his travels in Asia.

CHAPTER 12:
Cultural Celebrations

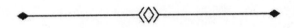

Fact 265: In India, the festival of Holi is celebrated by throwing colored powder at each other and dancing under water sprinklers. It's a vibrant party of colors!

Fact 266: Mexico's Day of the Dead is a cheerful celebration where families honor their ancestors with bright marigolds, sugar skulls, and festive parades.

Fact 267: The Chinese New Year, also known as the Spring Festival, involves giving red envelopes with money for good luck and setting off fireworks to scare away bad spirits.

Fact 268: In Japan, Children's Day is celebrated by flying carp-shaped kites called "koinobori." The carp are symbols of strength and success.

Fact 269: Spain has a tomato-throwing festival called La Tomatina, where thousands of people have a massive tomato fight just for fun!

Fact 270: The Jewish holiday Hanukkah is celebrated by lighting candles on a menorah for eight nights to remember an ancient miracle of oil that lasted longer than expected.

Fact 271: On Bastille Day in France, people celebrate with fireworks, parades, and parties to remember the French Revolution, which was a big step toward democracy.

Fact 272: In Brazil, the Carnival is celebrated with huge parades, samba music, and dazzling costumes that sparkle brighter than a sunny day at the beach.

Fact 273: Eid al-Fitr is a Muslim holiday that marks the end of Ramadan, a month of fasting, and is celebrated with feasts, gifts, and new clothes.

Fact 274: The United States celebrates Independence Day on July 4th with fireworks, barbecues, and patriotic parades.

Fact 275: Diwali, known as the festival of lights in Hinduism, celebrates the victory of good over evil with lamps, fireworks, and sweets.

Fact 276: In Scotland, people celebrate Hogmanay on New Year's Eve with bonfires and a tradition called "first-footing," where the first person to enter a home after midnight brings good fortune.

Fact 277: During the Lantern Festival in China, people release lanterns into the sky while guessing riddles written on the lanterns.

Fact 278: Mardi Gras, especially famous in New Orleans, is celebrated with masked balls and colorful parades. People often catch beads and other trinkets thrown from the floats.

Fact 279: In Turkey, National Sovereignty and Children's Day is celebrated on April 23rd, where children take seats in the Turkish Parliament to symbolically govern the country for one day.

Fact 280: The Canadian National Indigenous Peoples Day on June 21st honors the cultures and contributions of the First Nations, Inuit, and Métis peoples.

Fact 281: In South Korea, the first day of the Lunar New Year is called Seollal, and people play traditional games, wear hanboks (traditional clothing), and eat rice cake soup.

Fact 282: During the Midsummer festival in Sweden, people dance around a maypole, wear flower crowns, and enjoy the longest day of the year.

Fact 283: In Ethiopia, the Timkat Festival celebrates the Epiphany with people dressing in white, carrying colorful umbrellas, and parading through the streets.

Fact 284: The Maori of New Zealand celebrate Matariki, the Maori New Year, by watching the rise of the Pleiades star cluster and remembering those who have passed.

Fact 285: In Italy, during the Venice Carnival, people wear elaborate masks and costumes to take part in grand balls and gondola parades.

Fact 286: On St. Lucia's Day in Sweden, girls dress as "Lucia brides" in a white gown with a red sash and a crown of candles to bring light to the darkest time of the year.

Fact 287: The United Kingdom celebrates Guy Fawkes Night with bonfires and fireworks to remember the failed Gunpowder Plot of 1605.

Fact 288: The Songkran Festival in Thailand marks the Thai New Year with a country-wide water fight, symbolizing the washing away of bad luck.

CHAPTER 13:
Amazing Athletes

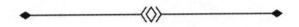

Fact 289: Usain Bolt, from Jamaica, holds the record for the fastest human sprint, clocking in at 9.58 seconds for the 100-meter dash. That's quicker than a cheetah... for a very short time!

Fact 290: In gymnastics, Simone Biles has a move named after her because she was the first to land it in competition—a double layout with a half twist!

Fact 291: Michael Phelps, the swimming superstar, has won more Olympic medals than anyone else in history, with a total of 28!

Fact 292: The youngest Olympian ever was Dimitrios Loundras, who competed in gymnastics at the 1896 Olympics at just 10 years old.

Fact 293: Serena Williams won her first major championship at 17 and has racked up 23 Grand Slam singles titles, one of the all-time highest in tennis.

Fact 294: In soccer, Marta Vieira da Silva from Brazil holds the record for the most goals scored at FIFA Women's World Cup tournaments, netting 17 in total.

Fact 295: Shaquille O'Neal, one of the most dominant basketball players ever, wore size 22 shoes—that's almost as long as a ruler!

Fact 296: Yusra Mardini, a Syrian swimmer, competed in the Olympics as part of the Refugee Olympic Team and previously saved lives by swimming a sinking boat to safety for three hours.

Fact 297: In 2016, Katie Ledecky, an American swimmer, won the 800-meter freestyle by over 11 seconds, which is like an eternity in swimming races!

Fact 298: The record for the most goals scored in a single professional soccer match is held by Stephan Stanis from France, scoring 16 goals for his team in 1942.

Fact 299: Babe Didrikson Zaharias was an amazing all-around athlete who won two gold medals in track and field at the 1932 Olympics and later became a champion golfer.

Fact 300: Lionel Messi, an Argentine soccer legend, was so skilled that at the age of 24, he became Barcelona's all-time top scorer.

Fact 301: Ma Long, a table tennis player from China, has been ranked world number 1 for a total of 64 months, the most by any male player in the history of the sport.

Fact 302: Takeru Kobayashi revolutionized competitive eating by downing 50 hot dogs in 12 minutes, doubling the previous record.

Fact 303: In cricket, Sachin Tendulkar from India scored 100 centuries in international play, which is considered a gigantic achievement in the sport.

Fact 304: The highest jump ever recorded by a horse in competition was 2.47 meters (8 feet 1 inch), achieved by Huaso, ridden by Captain Alberto Larraguibel from Chile, in 1949.

Fact 305: Wilt Chamberlain scored 100 points in a single NBA basketball game, setting a record that has stood since 1962.

Fact 306: Nadia Comaneci, a Romanian gymnast, scored the first perfect 10 in Olympic gymnastics during the 1976 Montreal Games.

Fact 307: In baseball, Nolan Ryan threw pitches regularly above 100 mph and holds the record for the most strikeouts—a whopping 5,714!

Fact 308: Florence Griffith Joyner, nicknamed "Flo Jo," set the world records in women's 100m and 200m in 1988, and they still stand today.

Fact 309: At the age of 13, Sky Brown became Britain's youngest Olympic medalist by taking bronze in skateboarding at the Tokyo 2020 Games.

Fact 310: Tony Hawk, a skateboarding legend, was the first to land a 900-degree aerial spin in competition, which means he turned around two and a half times!

Fact 311: The longest recorded tennis match took 11 hours and 5 minutes over three days, with John Isner defeating Nicolas Mahut at Wimbledon in 2010.

Fact 312: Chess prodigy Judit Polgar became the youngest ever grandmaster at age 15, breaking a record previously held by Bobby Fischer.

CHAPTER 14:
Technological Triumphs

Fact 313: The first computer was called the ENIAC and was as big as a classroom, but less powerful than a modern calculator!

Fact 314: Did you know the World Wide Web was invented by Tim Berners-Lee in 1989? That's not too long ago!

Fact 315: Mobile phones used to be huge; in the 1980s, they were the size of a brick and had giant antennas.

Fact 316: The first video game, created in the 1950s, was a simple tennis game similar to the classic "Pong" that came out two decades later.

Fact 317: Robots aren't just science fiction! The Mars Rovers are robots exploring Mars, sending back information to Earth.

Fact 318: Kodak created the first digital camera in 1975, but it was only 0.01 megapixels. Today's cameras can capture photos with over 100 megapixels!

Fact 319: GPS is a system of satellites that helps us find our way. It can tell you exactly where you are on Earth!

Fact 320: The first ever message sent on the internet was "LO." It was supposed to be "LOGIN," but the computer crashed after just two letters.

Fact 321: The original Nintendo Entertainment System (NES) was released in 1985 and changed video games forever with characters like Mario and Zelda.

Fact 322: In 2004, Facebook started in a college dorm room. Now, it's one of the biggest social media platforms on the planet.

Fact 323: The first smartphone was created by IBM in 1992 and was called Simon; it could even send emails.

Fact 324: Drones are used for all sorts of things, from taking photos to helping farmers check on their crops from the sky.

Fact 325: 3D printing can make all sorts of things, even houses and prosthetic limbs!

Fact 326: Virtual Reality (VR) lets you explore whole new worlds without leaving your room, using just a special headset.

Fact 327: The first electric car was built in the 1830s, well before cars with gasoline engines became popular.

Fact 328: Blockchain technology, best known for supporting cryptocurrencies like Bitcoin, provides a secure and transparent way to record transactions. Its potential extends beyond finance into areas like supply chain management, voting systems, and secure record-keeping.

Fact 329: In 1969, the first humans landed on the Moon, and they used computers less powerful than your smartphone to get there.

Fact 330: The first transatlantic telephone cable was laid in 1956 and could only handle 36 calls at a time.

Fact 331: Before streaming services, people rented movies from stores, and if you forgot to rewind the VHS tape, you might get a fine!

Fact 332: Self-driving cars are being tested on roads today. They use sensors and computers to see the road and make decisions.

Fact 333: The earliest form of writing, cuneiform, was developed by the Sumerians over 5,000 years ago. Now, we type on keyboards!

Fact 334: Credit cards have been around since the 1950s, but now we can pay with just a tap using smartphones or smartwatches.

Fact 335: Video calls were once a thing of sci-fi movies. Now, people around the world video chat every day with apps like Skype and Zoom.

Fact 336: Quantum computers, still in the experimental phase, promise to solve complex problems millions of times faster than current computers.

CHAPTER 15:
Remarkable Record Breakers

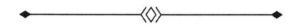

Fact 337: The world's tallest man ever recorded was Robert Wadlow, who grew to be 8 feet 11 inches tall!

Fact 338: The largest pizza ever made was in Rome, Italy, and it covered more than 13,580 square feet – that's as big as two soccer fields!

Fact 339: Did you know the longest fingernails on a pair of hands ever measured over 28 feet in total? That's longer than a school bus!

Fact 340: The longest marathon playing a board game was 61 hours and 2 minutes. Imagine playing Monopoly for that long!

Fact 341: A cat named Stubbs was the honorary mayor of a small town in Alaska for 20 years. He was pawsitively a good leader!

Fact 342: The most jelly beans eaten in one minute with chopsticks is 65. Talk about a sweet challenge!

Fact 343: The most people brushing their teeth simultaneously is 26,382. That's a lot of sparkling smiles!

Fact 344: The longest human tunnel traveled through by a skateboarding dog was 30 people. That's one talented pup!

Fact 345: The largest gathering of people dressed as penguins was 373. It was a real-life penguin party!

Fact 346: The world record for the largest bubble gum bubble blown is 20 inches in diameter – that's as big as a basketball!

Fact 347: A snail named Archie was the fastest ever, racing at 0.03 miles per hour. Slow and steady wins the race?

Fact 348: The most steps walked by a dog balancing a glass of water is 10. What a careful canine!

Fact 349: The largest collection of teddy bears is over 20,000. That's a lot of fuzzy friends!

Fact 350: The most leapfrog jumps in 30 seconds by a team of two is 32. Hop to it!

Fact 351: The longest time spent living in a tree is over 2 years. Now that's a real treehouse!

Fact 352: The fastest time to type the alphabet on a tablet is 3.43 seconds. Quick fingers!

Fact 353: The most spoons balanced on a human face is 31. Don't try this at dinner!

Fact 354: The highest score on "Space Invaders" is 110,510 points. That's a lot of alien invasions stopped!

Fact 355: The largest collection of toothpaste tubes is over 3,000. Squeezing them all might be a bit much!

Fact 356: The longest bike ever ridden was over 135 feet long. Imagine trying to turn the corner with that!

Fact 357: The most stairs climbed while balancing a person on the head is 90. That's a tall order!

Fact 358: The most ice cream scoops balanced on a cone is 121. Just hope it doesn't melt!

Fact 359: The most consecutive pogo stick jumps are 88,047. Boing, boing, boing!

Fact 360: The longest time spinning a basketball on a toothbrush is over 22 minutes. That's some serious dental dexterity!

CHAPTER 16:
Art and Music Marvels

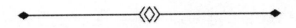

Fact 361: The Mona Lisa, painted by Leonardo da Vinci, has her own mailbox at the Louvre Museum because she receives so many letters!

Fact 362: The famous "Sunflowers" painting by Vincent van Gogh was part of a series; he painted seven different versions of sunflowers.

Fact 363: The largest canvas painting ever created measured 17,176 square feet, which is about one-third the size of a football field!

Fact 364: Ludwig van Beethoven started losing his hearing in his 20s, but he still composed some of the world's most famous music.

Fact 365: The children's song "Twinkle, Twinkle, Little Star" has the same melody as the "Alphabet Song" and "Baa, Baa, Black Sheep." They all come from a French tune composed by Mozart!

Fact 366: Pablo Picasso could draw before he could walk, and his first word was "pencil" in Spanish.

Fact 367: The first guitar was created in ancient Egypt over 3,500 years ago – that's an oldie!

Fact 368: The world's largest sculpture is the Spring Temple Buddha in China, standing over 500 feet tall.

Fact 369: The White House has its own concert hall where presidents can listen to performances right at home.

Fact 370: Salvador Dalí once arrived at an art exhibition in a limousine filled with cauliflower.

Fact 371: Some musical compositions are so long that they take hundreds of years to play. One such piece by John Cage is set to last 639 years!

Fact 372: Frida Kahlo, known for her self-portraits, started painting after she was injured in a bus accident, which gave her a lot of time to practice her art.

Fact 373: The Sydney Opera House has over 1 million roof tiles, and they're all white!

Fact 374: An artist named Keith Haring liked to draw on empty advertising panels in New York's subway stations using white chalk.

Fact 375: The world's largest functioning guitar is 43 feet long, which is almost as long as a bowling lane.

Fact 376: Some violins, called Stradivarius violins made in the 1700s, are worth millions of dollars today.

Fact 377: The world's longest music video is Michael Jackson's "Ghosts," which is 39 minutes long.

Fact 378: The famous sculpture, the Statue of Liberty, was a gift from France to the United States and is made of copper.

Fact 379: In Renaissance times, artists would often paint over their own work, so there are hidden paintings beneath some famous artworks.

Fact 380: The oldest known musical instruments are flutes made from bird bones and mammoth ivory, found in Germany and believed to be over 40,000 years old.

Fact 381: The Beatles hold the record for the most number-one hits on the Billboard Hot 100 chart.

Fact 382: Claude Monet, famous for his Water Lilies series, actually had a huge garden and pond where he would paint them.

Fact 383: The song "Happy Birthday to You" is the most recognized song in the English language.

Fact 384: Banksy is a mysterious street artist known for his graffiti art, but nobody knows his true identity!

CHAPTER 17:
Environmental Insights

Fact 385: Rainforests are home to more than half of the world's plant and animal species, even though they cover less than 2% of Earth's surface.

Fact 386: The Great Barrier Reef is the largest living structure on Earth and can be seen from space!

Fact 387: Biodiversity is a term that means the variety of life in a particular habitat or ecosystem, and more biodiversity means a healthier environment.

Fact 388: The Amazon Rainforest produces about 20% of the world's oxygen, earning it the nickname "the lungs of the Earth."

Fact 389: Solar panels can generate electricity by converting sunlight into energy, and they don't produce air pollution.

Fact 390: Bees are super important because they pollinate plants, which helps fruits, nuts, and vegetables to grow.

Fact 391: The tallest tree in the world is a coast redwood in California, standing at 379 feet tall—that's about as tall as a 35-story building!

Fact 392: Wind farms use giant turbines to turn wind into electricity without any harmful emissions.

Fact 393: The world's largest land animal, the African elephant, helps to maintain forest and savanna ecosystems by dispersing seeds in their dung.

Fact 394: Recycling one aluminum can save enough energy to power a TV for three hours.

Fact 395: Sea otters play a crucial role in their environment by eating sea urchins, which helps kelp forests to thrive.

Fact 396: The blue whale's heart is so big, a small child could swim through its arteries.

Fact 397: A single tree can absorb as much as 48 pounds of carbon dioxide per year, helping to combat climate change.

Fact 398: Coral reefs protect coastlines from storms and erosion, provide jobs for local communities, and offer opportunities for recreation.

Fact 399: Earthworms enrich the soil by breaking down dead plant material, which makes it easier for plants to get nutrients.

Fact 400: The Venus flytrap, a carnivorous plant, gets some of its nutrients by trapping and digesting insects.

Fact 401: The energy it takes to produce one plastic bottle can fill that bottle one-quarter full with oil.

Fact 402: A keystone species is one that has a disproportionately large effect on its environment relative to its abundance, like the gray wolf in Yellowstone National Park.

Fact 403: The Arctic is warming twice as fast as the rest of the planet, which affects global weather patterns.

Fact 404: Mangrove forests along coastlines act as natural barriers, reducing the force of waves and helping to prevent soil erosion.

Fact 405: A mature leafy tree produces as much oxygen in a season as 10 people inhale in a year.

Fact 406: Over 8 million tons of plastic are dumped into the ocean each year, which is like dumping a garbage truck full of plastic every minute.

Fact 407: Bioluminescence is the ability of certain organisms to glow, which can be found in some algae, jellyfish, worms, and fish in the deep sea.

Fact 408: The Peregrine falcon, the fastest bird, helps control populations of pigeons and other small birds, balancing the ecosystem.

CHAPTER 18:
Powerful Earth Forces

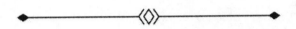

Fact 409: Volcanoes can form new land! The Hawaiian Islands were formed by volcanic eruptions that happened under the ocean over millions of years.

Fact 410: Earthquakes happen when two blocks of the earth suddenly slip past one another. The surface where they slip is called the fault or fault plane.

Fact 411: The Ring of Fire is a huge area in the Pacific Ocean where many earthquakes and volcanic eruptions occur, and it's shaped like a giant ring.

Fact 412: The Earth's crust is made of pieces called tectonic plates, which are always moving, but usually just a few inches each year.

Fact 413: Lava is the molten rock that comes out of a volcano during an eruption, and it can flow really fast—up to 40 miles per hour!

Fact 414: The world's largest volcano, Mauna Loa in Hawaii, is so big that it's even bigger than the whole state of Rhode Island.

Fact 415: Earthquakes can permanently change the Earth's surface; after the 2010 earthquake in Chile, the city of Concepción moved 10 feet to the west!

Fact 416: A tsunami is a huge wave usually caused by an earthquake under the sea, and in deep water, it can travel as fast as a jet plane.

Fact 417: Some lakes are formed by volcanoes. When a volcano's crater stops erupting, it can fill with water and become a lake.

Fact 418: There are about 1,500 active volcanoes on the Earth, and around 500 have erupted in historical times.

Fact 419: The Richter scale measures the strength of earthquakes. A small increase in number means a huge increase in shaking!

Fact 420: Magma is the name for molten rock while it's still under the Earth's surface; it's only called lava after it erupts.

Fact 421: A geyser is a type of hot spring that shoots water into the air. It's caused by hot volcanic rocks heating water underground.

Fact 422: The deepest part of the Earth's crust that humans have ever drilled is the Kola Superdeep Borehole in Russia, which is over 7 miles deep.

Fact 423: The most deadly volcanic eruption in history was Mount Tambora in Indonesia in 1815, which caused a year without summer due to the ash it spread in the atmosphere.

Fact 424: The San Andreas Fault in California is one of the most famous faults in the world, partly because it's the boundary between two major tectonic plates.

Fact 425: A volcanic eruption in 1783 in Iceland released so much ash and gas that it cooled the Earth and caused famine in Europe.

Fact 426: Earth's largest earthquake ever recorded was in Chile in 1960 with a magnitude of 9.5, which is super powerful.

Fact 427: Pumice is a type of volcanic rock that can float on water because it's full of air bubbles.

Fact 428: Hotspots are places within the Earth's mantle where rocks melt to generate magma. The Hawaiian Islands are sitting on a hotspot, which is why they have active volcanoes.

Fact 429: The Pacific Plate is the world's largest tectonic plate, covering an area larger than the continent of Asia!

Fact 430: Volcanic ash can travel thousands of miles; ash from an eruption in Indonesia once reached the African island of Madagascar.

Fact 431: Old Faithful is a famous geyser in Yellowstone National Park, USA. It erupts almost every 90 minutes.

Fact 432: Sulfur from volcanoes can create brilliant blue flames, like those seen at the Kawah Ijen volcano in Indonesia.

CHAPTER 19:
Mythical Creatures and Legends

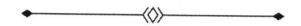

Fact 433: Dragons are legendary creatures known across the world. In China, dragons are seen as wise and good, quite different from the fierce dragons in European tales.

Fact 434: The Loch Ness Monster, affectionately known as Nessie, is a famous creature said to inhabit Loch Ness in Scotland. Despite many searches, Nessie's existence remains a fun mystery.

Fact 435: Unicorns, horses with a single spiraled horn, have been a symbol of purity and grace in many cultures, and they were believed to have magical powers.

Fact 436: Mermaids and mermen, half-human, half-fish creatures, are part of folklore in many parts of the world, from Europe to Africa and Asia.

Fact 437: The Phoenix is a bird from Greek mythology that bursts into flames when it dies, only to be reborn from its ashes.

Fact 438: Bigfoot, also known as Sasquatch, is a big, hairy creature that some people believe lives in the forests of North America.

Fact 439: In Norse mythology, Thor is the god of thunder, lightning, storms, oak trees, strength, and the protection of mankind. He has a powerful hammer named Mjolnir.

Fact 440: The Kraken is a legendary sea monster of giant proportions that is said to dwell off the coasts of Norway and Greenland.

Fact 441: Pegasus is a winged horse from Greek mythology and is known for being the child of Poseidon, the god of the sea.

Fact 442: The Chupacabra, whose name means 'goat-sucker' in Spanish, is a creature said to live in parts of the Americas, where it preys on livestock.

Fact 443: Fairies are small, magical beings with wings, known to be mischievous, and they come from European folklore.

Fact 444: The Minotaur, a creature with the head of a bull and the body of a man, was a famous monster from Greek mythology.

Fact 445: Anubis is an ancient Egyptian god with the head of a jackal, who helped to guide the souls of the dead to the afterlife.

Fact 446: Banshees are female spirits from Irish folklore, and hearing their wailing is a sign that someone is about to die.

Fact 447: In Australian Aboriginal mythology, the Rainbow Serpent is a great, powerful, and benevolent creature that is a symbol of life, water, and regeneration.

Fact 448: The Yeti, or the Abominable Snowman, is a legendary ape-like creature said to live in the Himalayan mountains.

Fact 449: Griffins, with the body of a lion and the head and wings of an eagle, are mythical creatures known as symbols of divine power.

Fact 450: The Japanese Kappa is a water creature that is part frog, part turtle, and it's known for being both mischievous and occasionally helpful.

Fact 451: Medusa, with hair of snakes, could turn anyone who looked directly at her into stone, according to Greek mythology.

Fact 452: Leprechauns are a type of fairy in Irish folklore, usually depicted as little bearded men, wearing coats and hats who partake in mischief.

Fact 453: The Hydra was a multi-headed serpent in Greek mythology; when one head was cut off, two more would grow back in its place.

Fact 454: The Basilisk, known as the King of Serpents, is said to be so venomous that it leaves a wide trail of deadly venom in its wake.

Fact 455: Selkies are mythical beings found in Scottish, Irish, and Faroese folklore who can transform from seals to humans by shedding their skin.

Fact 456: In Hindu mythology, Garuda is a divine eagle-like sun bird and the king of birds. He is a creature of immense power and is the vehicle (vahana) of Lord Vishnu.

CHAPTER 20:
Food Facts

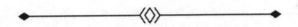

Fact 457: In Japan, square watermelons are grown by farmers for easier stack and store, and they're made by placing them in square, tempered glass cases while they're growing on the vine.

Fact 458: The world's most expensive pizza, named Louis XIII, costs $12,000 and takes 72 hours to make. It's topped with three types of caviar, lobster from Norway, Cilento, bufala mozzarella cheese, and pink Australian sea salt.

Fact 459: Chocolate was once used as currency by the ancient Mayans and Aztecs. It was so valuable that people would trade cacao beans for goods or services.

Fact 460: The fear of peanut butter sticking to the roof of the mouth is called Arachibutyrophobia. It might sound funny, but it's a real concern for some!

Fact 461: Honey never spoils. Archaeologists have found pots of honey in ancient Egyptian tombs that are over 3,000 years old and still good to eat.

Fact 462: The largest fruit in the world is the jackfruit, which can grow up to 100 pounds and is found in parts of Southeast Asia, Brazil, and Africa.

Fact 463: In Sweden, there's a traditional dish called Surströmming, which is fermented herring. It has such a strong smell that it's usually eaten outdoors.

Fact 464: Apples float in water because 25% of their volume is air. This is why they bob up and down when you put them in a tub for apple bobbing on Halloween.

Fact 465: Ketchup was sold in the 1830s as medicine for indigestion. It wasn't until later that it became a popular condiment.

Fact 466: There's a fruit by the name of 'Miracle Berry' that makes sour foods taste sweet. After eating it, lemons can taste like sugary lemonade.

Fact 467: The biggest chocolate bar ever made weighed 5,792 kg (12,770 lb). It was created by Thorntons PLC in the UK on September 7, 2011.

Fact 468: The stinky fruit Durian from Southeast Asia smells so bad that it's banned from some public places, like hotels and trains, in Singapore.

Fact 469: Carrots weren't originally orange; they were purple, red, white, and yellow. The orange carrot was developed and stabilized by Dutch growers in the 16th and 17th centuries.

Fact 470: Saffron is the most expensive spice in the world. It comes from the saffron crocus flower, and it takes about 75,000 blossoms to produce just one pound of saffron spice.

Fact 471: The hottest chili pepper in the world is the Carolina Reaper. It's so hot that it can cause skin burns if not handled properly.

Fact 472: The world's largest bowl of pasta was made in California in 2015 and weighed 7,900kg. That's a lot of spaghetti!

Fact 473: In 17th century Europe, a pineapple was so expensive that you could rent one for a night to take to a party for bragging rights.

Fact 474: A single spaghetti noodle is called a "spaghetto," and a single ravioli is called a "raviolo."

Fact 475: The first ice cream cone was produced in 1904 at the World's Fair in St. Louis, Missouri. Ice cream vendors ran out of dishes and got help from a nearby waffle vendor who rolled his waffles into cones!

Fact 476: Fortune cookies are not traditionally Chinese. They were actually invented in America, and in China, they are seen as a symbol of American cuisine.

Fact 477: In ancient times, people used bread to wipe their plates clean and then eat it. This practice was called "trenchering."

Fact 478: A cluster of bananas is called a hand, and a single banana is called a finger.

Fact 479: In South Korea, there's a special kind of kimchi made with whole cabbages and stuffed with all sorts of ingredients. It's called "tongbaechu-kimchi."

Fact 480: Gummi bears were invented by a German company called Haribo in 1922. The creator, Hans Riegel, was inspired by the dancing bears featured in European festivals and markets.

CHAPTER 21:
Wonders of Weather

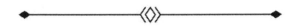

Fact 481: The highest temperature ever recorded on Earth was 134°F (56.7°C) in Death Valley, California, on July 10, 1913. Imagine the sun being so hot that you could fry an egg on the sidewalk!

Fact 482: Snowflakes come in all sorts of intricate patterns, but no two snowflakes are exactly the same. They're like tiny, icy fingerprints from the sky!

Fact 483: Lightning can get really hot—about five times hotter than the surface of the sun! A single bolt can reach temperatures of approximately 53,540°F (30,000°C).

Fact 484: Tornadoes can rip through a place with winds up to 300 miles per hour. That's as fast as racecars zooming around a track!

Fact 485: The wettest place on Earth is Mawsynram in India, where it can rain over 467 inches in a year. That's a lot of umbrellas and raincoats!

Fact 486: Have you ever heard of a haboob? It's a massive dust storm that happens in dry regions, and it can block out the sun completely.

Fact 487: The coldest temperature ever recorded was -128.6°F (-89.2°C) at the Soviet Union's Vostok Station in

Antarctica on July 21, 1983. That's colder than the freezer where you keep your ice cream!

Fact 488: A hurricane can dump 2.4 trillion gallons (9 trillion liters) of rain a day. That's enough water to fill over 3,600 Olympic-sized swimming pools!

Fact 489: Thundersnow is a rare kind of thunderstorm with snow falling as the primary precipitation instead of rain. It's like a snowball fight with a soundtrack of thunder!

Fact 490: Did you know that clouds can weigh a lot? A cumulus cloud can weigh up to 1.1 million pounds—that's the weight of about 100 elephants!

Fact 491: Waterspouts are tornadoes that happen over water. They can suck up small creatures from the sea and rain them down onto land.

Fact 492: Ball lightning is a strange phenomenon where lightning forms a glowing, spherical shape and can float or bounce around in the air.

Fact 493: The Atacama Desert in South America is so dry that some parts of it have never had rain. It's like a giant sandbox that stretches for miles and miles!

Fact 494: In the Philippines, the weather is so consistently hot that there are only two seasons: wet and dry. No need for winter coats here!

Fact 495: The Aurora Borealis, also known as the Northern Lights, is a natural light display caused by the collision of charged particles directed by Earth's magnetic field.

Fact 496: A single lightning bolt has enough energy to toast about 100,000 slices of bread. Talk about a supercharged snack!

Fact 497: Frost flowers are delicate ice formations that look like flowers and grow on frozen surfaces. They're not plants but are actually ice crystals that form in certain conditions.

Fact 498: Some hurricanes can become so large that they can be seen from space. Astronauts have spotted these massive storms swirling on Earth's surface.

Fact 499: The Great Red Spot on Jupiter is actually a gigantic storm that's been raging for at least 400 years. It's so big that three Earths could fit inside it!

Fact 500: A 'sun dog' is a halo that can appear around the sun, making it look as if there are three suns in the sky. It's caused by ice crystals in the atmosphere.

Fact 501: The wind doesn't make a sound until it blows against objects—trees, windows, or even the strings of a wind chime. Otherwise, it's just moving air in silence.

Fact 502: "Diamond Dust" is a ground-level cloud composed of tiny ice crystals. It's like a glittery mist that doesn't fall as precipitation.

Fact 503: In Antarctica, the wind can create snow sculptures called "sastrugi," which are sharp irregular grooves on the snow surface.

Fact 504: There's a rare phenomenon called "fire rainbows," which occur when sunlight reflects through ice crystals in high cirrus clouds. Despite their name, they don't have any fire and are not related to rainbows.

CHAPTER 22:
Cosmic Mysteries

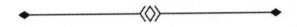

Fact 505: Black holes are so powerful that not even light can escape their grasp. If you shined a flashlight into a black hole, the light would just get sucked in!

Fact 506: Dark matter is invisible, and it doesn't emit, absorb, or reflect light. Even though we can't see it, scientists think it makes up about 27% of the universe.

Fact 507: Neutron stars, which are the leftovers from when a star explodes, are so dense that a sugar-cube-sized amount of neutron-star material would weigh about a billion tons on Earth.

Fact 508: The Milky Way galaxy is on a collision course with the Andromeda galaxy. But don't worry—it won't happen for about 4 billion years.

Fact 509: Some galaxies are so far away that the light we see from them today actually left those galaxies billions of years ago. So, when you look at them, you're seeing into the past!

Fact 510: Quasars are the brightest objects in the universe and are thought to be the centers of very young galaxies. They can outshine an entire galaxy of billions of stars.

Fact 511: The largest known star, UY Scuti, is so big that if it were placed in our solar system, it would swallow up everything up to the orbit of Jupiter.

Fact 512: White holes are theoretical opposites of black holes where nothing can enter, but light and matter could come out. However, scientists have never observed one.

Fact 513: The Voyager 1 spacecraft, launched in 1977, is the farthest human-made object from Earth. It's now in interstellar space, sending back data from beyond our solar system.

Fact 514: There is a giant cloud of alcohol in space. It's not the kind you can drink, but it contains enough alcohol to fill 400 trillion trillion pints of beer.

Fact 515: The Boomerang Nebula is the coldest known place in the universe, with temperatures lower than the background radiation after the Big Bang.

Fact 516: A light-year is the distance light travels in a year, about 5.88 trillion miles (9.46 trillion kilometers). It's like driving around Earth's equator 236 million times!

Fact 517: Black holes can spin at nearly the speed of light, causing the space around them to twist.

Fact 518: Pulsars are neutron stars that emit beams of radiation like a lighthouse. Some spin hundreds of times per second.

Fact 519: If you could compress Earth down to the size of a small marble, it would become a black hole.

Fact 520: There's a planet made of diamonds called 55 Cancri e. It's twice the size of Earth and eight times its mass.

Fact 521: Scientists have found a giant reservoir of water vapor in space which holds 140 trillion times the amount of water in Earth's oceans.

Fact 522: The Cosmic Microwave Background is the afterglow radiation from the Big Bang and is the oldest light in the universe that we can see.

Fact 523: Wormholes are theoretical passages through space-time that could create shortcuts for long journeys across the universe.

Fact 524: Some dwarf galaxies are just a few hundred light-years across, which is tiny compared to our Milky Way, which is about 100,000 light-years wide.

Fact 525: Magnetars are neutron stars with the strongest known magnetic fields in the universe. They are so strong they could strip the information from a credit card from 100,000 miles away.

Fact 526: The Great Attractor is a gravitational anomaly in intergalactic space that reveals the existence of a local supercluster, drawing galaxies toward it.

Fact 527: The Hubble Space Telescope can look at a patch of seemingly empty space and find thousands of galaxies, each containing billions of stars.

Fact 528: There's a giant exoplanet where it rains molten glass, sideways, in 7,000 kilometer-per-hour winds. This planet is called HD 189733b.

CHAPTER 23:
Ancient Civilizations

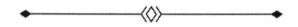

Fact 529: Ancient Egyptians loved board games. One popular game was Senet, which was played for over 2000 years!

Fact 530: The Great Pyramid of Giza was the tallest man-made structure for over 3,800 years. It's made of about 2.3 million stone blocks!

Fact 531: Romans had a god for almost everything, even door hinges! His name was Cardea.

Fact 532: Ancient Greek children played with toys similar to ones you might have, like dolls, yo-yos, and spinning tops.

Fact 533: In ancient Rome, the Colosseum could seat up to 50,000 spectators for gladiator fights and other events.

Fact 534: The Mayans from Central America were great at math and astronomy. They had one of the most accurate calendars in ancient times.

Fact 535: In ancient Egypt, pharaohs were often buried with their most treasured items, which they believed they could use in the afterlife.

Fact 536: The ancient city of Rome was eight times more densely populated than modern-day New York City!

Fact 537: The Greeks had a machine called the Antikythera mechanism, which could predict eclipses and keep track of calendars. It's like an ancient computer!

Fact 538: The world's first library was built by the Assyrian ruler Ashurbanipal in Nineveh, now modern-day Iraq.

Fact 539: Ancient Egyptians used a writing system called hieroglyphics, which used more than 700 different symbols.

Fact 540: The Incas in South America built a vast empire without the use of wheels, iron tools, or even written language.

Fact 541: Ancient Egyptians invented toothpaste, which could include ingredients like eggshells and ashes.

Fact 542: In ancient China, people believed in a dragon that ate the sun during a solar eclipse. They made loud noises to scare it away!

Fact 543: The Olympic Games started in ancient Greece in 776 BC. Only free men who spoke Greek could compete.

Fact 544: Ancient Romans had central heating in their homes and public baths through a system called a hypocaust.

Fact 545: The Hanging Gardens of Babylon were one of the Seven Wonders of the Ancient World, and some think they might have been a rooftop garden.

Fact 546: Some ancient civilizations, like the Indus Valley, had toilets and sewer systems in their homes over 5,000 years ago.

Fact 547: Ancient Egyptians often kept cats as pets, believing they brought good luck and could ward off evil spirits.

Fact 548: Greek philosopher Plato wrote about a lost city called Atlantis, which has inspired treasure hunters for centuries.

Fact 549: In ancient Egypt, scribes didn't have to pay taxes or join the military, which made their job very desirable.

Fact 550: The Aztecs in Mexico created floating gardens called "chinampas" to grow crops on the surface of lakes.

Fact 551: In ancient Rome, purple clothing was reserved for emperors and senators because purple dye was extremely expensive.

Fact 552: The ancient Olympic athletes competed naked to honor the Greek god Zeus, and women were not allowed to watch the games.

CHAPTER 24:
Famous Explorers

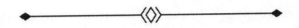

Fact 553: Marco Polo, a Venetian explorer, traveled to Asia and lived in China for 17 years. He even worked for the great emperor Kublai Khan!

Fact 554: Christopher Columbus made four voyages across the Atlantic Ocean from Spain, aiming to find a new route to Asia but instead stumbled upon the Americas in 1492.

Fact 555: Amelia Earhart was the first female aviator to fly solo across the Atlantic Ocean. She also wrote best-selling books about her flying adventures!

Fact 556: The famous British explorer James Cook mapped many areas from New Zealand to Hawaii in the Pacific Ocean and even reached the icy edges of Antarctica.

Fact 557: Sacagawea, a Lemhi Shoshone woman, helped Lewis and Clark on their expedition across the American West, serving as an interpreter and guide.

Fact 558: Ibn Battuta was a Moroccan explorer who traveled for nearly 30 years, covering over 120,000 kilometers (75,000 miles), possibly more than any other explorer in pre-modern history.

Fact 559: Ferdinand Magellan's expedition was the first to circumnavigate the Earth. Interestingly, Magellan didn't complete the journey himself as he died during the voyage.

Fact 560: Neil Armstrong wasn't just an astronaut; he was a space explorer. In 1969, he was the first person to walk on the moon, saying the famous words, "That's one small step for man, one giant leap for mankind."

Fact 561: Zheng He, a Chinese mariner, explorer, and fleet admiral, led several voyages that traversed the South China Sea and the Indian Ocean, reaching as far as East Africa.

Fact 562: Roald Amundsen was a tough Norwegian explorer who was the first to reach the South Pole in 1911. He even raced against another explorer, Robert Falcon Scott!

Fact 563: Daniel Boone was an American pioneer who explored and settled the area of Kentucky. It was considered the Wild West back in his day!

Fact 564: Jeanne Baret was the first woman to circumnavigate the globe, but she had to disguise herself as a man to join the voyage because women were not allowed on French naval ships at the time.

Fact 565: Sir Francis Drake was the first Englishman to circumnavigate the globe, and as a bonus, he was knighted by Queen Elizabeth I aboard his ship.

Fact 566: David Livingstone was a Scottish explorer in Africa. He went on a mission to find the source of the Nile River and had many adventures along the way.

Fact 567: Hernán Cortés was a Spanish Conquistador who led an expedition that caused the fall of the Aztec Empire. He brought back lots of gold and treasures to Spain.

Fact 568: Mary Kingsley was a British explorer who traveled alone through uncharted areas of West Africa in the late 1800s. She studied local customs and traded goods.

Fact 569: John Cabot was an Italian navigator and explorer, and his 1497 North American discovery was one of the earliest European explorations of the North American mainland.

Fact 570: The Lewis and Clark Expedition lasted from 1804 to 1806 and was the first American overland expedition to the Pacific coast and back.

Fact 571: Abel Tasman was a Dutch seafarer, explorer, and merchant. He was the first known European to reach the islands of Van Diemen's Land (now Tasmania) and New Zealand.

Fact 572: Vasco da Gama was a Portuguese explorer and the first European to reach India by sea. This route helped Portugal establish a long-lasting colonial empire in Asia.

Fact 573: Matthew Henson was an African American explorer best known for being the co-discoverer of the North Pole with Robert Peary in 1909.

Fact 574: Ernest Shackleton was a polar explorer who led three British expeditions to the Antarctic. His most famous was the Endurance expedition, where his ship was trapped and crushed by ice.

Fact 575: Ynes Mexia was a Mexican-American botanist and explorer who started her career at the age of 55. She collected over 145,000 specimens!

Fact 576: Alexander the Great was not only a king and a commander but also an explorer. He created one of the largest empires of the ancient world by the age of 30.

CHAPTER 25:
Incredible Insects

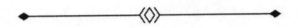

Fact 577: The honeybee communicates by dancing. Its movements can tell other bees where to find food!

Fact 578: Dragonflies are expert fliers. They can zip back and forth and even hover like a helicopter.

Fact 579: Did you know that ants have super strength? They can carry objects 50 times their own body weight!

Fact 580: A group of butterflies is called a flutter. And isn't that just the perfect name for it?

Fact 581: Ladybugs aren't just cute; they're also hungry aphid-eaters, making them great friends to gardeners.

Fact 582: The praying mantis can turn its head 180 degrees—that's like you looking backward without turning your body!

Fact 583: Some tropical spiders protect their young by making a "spider umbrella," using their bodies to shield them from rain.

Fact 584: Caterpillars have 12 eyes! Despite this, they can't see very well and just perceive light and dark.

Fact 585: Fireflies aren't flies at all; they are actually beetles that can light up due to a chemical reaction in their abdomens.

Fact 586: The longest insect in the world is the Chan's megastick, which can be over half a meter long (that's about the length of your arm!).

Fact 587: Grasshoppers have been around for 250 million years, which means they lived alongside dinosaurs.

Fact 588: The Atlas moth is one of the largest moths in the world, with a wingspan up to 11 inches (28 cm)—that's wider than a ruler!

Fact 589: Some ants can build bridges out of their bodies to cross water or gaps in leaves, working together as a team.

Fact 590: Cockroaches are famous for being tough—they've been around since the time of dinosaurs and can live for weeks without their heads!

Fact 591: A termite queen can lay up to 30,000 eggs in a single day. Talk about a busy mom!

Fact 592: The Goliath beetle is one of the heaviest insects on Earth. It can weigh as much as a quarter pounder hamburger!

Fact 593: Stick insects can camouflage themselves to look exactly like a twig, which helps them hide from hungry predators.

Fact 594: Fleas can jump over 100 times their own height. In human terms, that's like you leaping over a skyscraper!

Fact 595: There's a type of insect called a water strider that can walk on water, thanks to its super-long legs that spread out its weight.

Fact 596: The peacock butterfly can scare off predators with its wings that have big, eye-like spots. When it opens its wings, it looks like a much larger creature!

Fact 597: A dung beetle can roll up to 10 times its weight. Imagine pushing a ball of dung the size of a car!

Fact 598: Butterflies taste with their feet. They land on plants to taste them and see if their caterpillars can eat them.

Fact 599: Mosquitoes are attracted to the color blue twice as much as to any other color.

Fact 600: Some moths don't have stomachs. When they turn into moths, they can't eat and only live for a few days just to mate.

CHAPTER 26:
Magnificent Machines

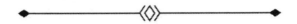

F act 601: The wheel, one of the oldest simple machines, was invented more than 5,000 years ago, and it's still rolling in all sorts of modern machines!

Fact 602: Clocks are machines that can measure time. The pendulum clock, invented in 1656, was the most accurate way to keep time for nearly 300 years.

Fact 603: Steam engines powered the first trains. They work by boiling water with coal to create steam, which then pushes pistons back and forth to move the train.

Fact 604: Robots in factories can work all day and night without getting tired. They help make cars, electronics, and even chocolates!

Fact 605: The first successful airplane, the Wright Flyer, flew in 1903. It only flew for 12 seconds, but it was a huge breakthrough in travel.

Fact 606: Space rovers, like the ones sent to Mars, are designed to drive over rocky alien terrain and can be controlled by scientists back on Earth.

Fact 607: The largest machine in the world is the Large Hadron Collider in Switzerland. It's a particle accelerator that's 17 miles (27 kilometers) in circumference.

Fact 608: The cotton gin, invented in 1793 by Eli Whitney, revolutionized the way cotton was harvested and processed.

Fact 609: Hydraulic machines use liquid power to do heavy lifting. Dump trucks and airplane controls use hydraulics to move large loads smoothly.

Fact 610: The first computers were so big they could fill an entire room, but now there are computers small enough to fit on your wrist, like a smartwatch!

Fact 611: Submarines can dive deep underwater by filling tanks with water to sink and then pushing it out with air to float back up.

Fact 612: Jet engines work by sucking in air, compressing it, mixing it with fuel, and then blasting it out the back to push the plane forward.

Fact 613: Some machines, called automata, are designed to follow a sequence of operations to give the appearance of moving on their own. They were the ancestors of robots.

Fact 614: The first digital camera was invented in 1975 and could only take black and white photographs.

Fact 615: 3D printers can make three-dimensional objects by adding material layer by layer, from toys to parts for machines, and even houses.

Fact 616: The Internet is actually a giant global network of computers, routers, and cables. It's like a worldwide web of machines talking to each other!

Fact 617: The tallest cranes can reach higher than the tallest buildings and are used to lift heavy items to great heights during construction.

Fact 618: The first vending machine was invented by Hero of Alexandria in the 1st century AD. It dispensed holy water when a coin was inserted.

Fact 619: Machines called escalators move people up and down floors in buildings. The first working escalator was installed in 1896 at Coney Island, New York.

Fact 620: The bicycle is a simple machine that gets you moving with just the push of your legs. The first chain-driven bicycle was invented in 1885.

Fact 621: Electric motors use magnets and electricity to spin around, which can then make other things move, like the wheels on a toy car or the fan above your head.

Fact 622: The first practical sewing machine was invented in 1829, which helped people make clothes much faster than sewing by hand.

Fact 623: Drones are like small helicopters with cameras that people can fly with remote controls to take pictures from the sky.

Fact 624: The deepest-diving submarine, the Trieste, reached the bottom of the Mariana Trench, the deepest part of the ocean, way back in 1960.

CHAPTER 27:
Underground Secrets

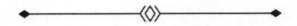

Fact 625: The deepest cave on Earth is the Veryovkina Cave in the country of Georgia, which goes down more than 7,257 feet (2,212 meters). That's over a mile straight down!

Fact 626: Caves can grow crystals. Mexico's Cave of the Crystals has some of the biggest natural crystals ever found, as tall as trees and as heavy as elephants.

Fact 627: The oldest human fossils ever discovered were found in Ethiopia. They're about 2.8 million years old!

Fact 628: Some caves have their own weather systems. The Cave of Winds in Colorado has strong air currents that can blow your hat off!

Fact 629: Archaeologists found the world's oldest known musical instruments—flutes—inside a cave in Germany. They're made from bird bones and mammoth ivory.

Fact 630: Lava tubes are underground tunnels formed by flowing lava. When the lava cools and hardens on the outside, it creates a natural pipe.

Fact 631: The world's longest underground river flows through the Yucatán Peninsula in Mexico. It's part of a network of flooded caverns called cenotes.

Fact 632: In Scotland, there's a secret underground city called Mary King's Close. In the 1600s, people actually lived down there!

Fact 633: "Ice caves" aren't just caves with ice inside. They're made entirely of ice, like the Eisriesenwelt Ice Cave in Austria, which is the largest in the world.

Fact 634: The Terracotta Army is a collection of thousands of clay soldiers buried underground in China to protect the first emperor in the afterlife.

Fact 635: In Turkey, the ancient underground city of Derinkuyu could shelter as many as 20,000 people. It had schools, churches, and food storage.

Fact 636: Mammoth Cave in Kentucky is the world's longest cave system, with more than 400 miles (640 kilometers) explored.

Fact 637: The Dead Sea Scrolls, some of the oldest known biblical manuscripts, were found hidden in caves near the Dead Sea.

Fact 638: Fossils of the Megalodon, a prehistoric shark bigger than a school bus, have been found all over the world, including deep under the ocean floor.

Fact 639: "Blue holes" are underwater caves or sinkholes, and they're called that because from above, they look like dark blue spots in the sea.

Fact 640: The Catacombs of Paris are underground tunnels that hold the remains of more than six million people.

Fact 641: In Slovenia, the Postojna Cave system is so big that it has its own railway for tourists to explore its chambers.

Fact 642: Ants can build huge underground colonies, sometimes going down 25 feet (7.6 meters) or more and housing millions of ants.

Fact 643: The deepest part of the ocean is called the Mariana Trench. If you put Mount Everest in there, its peak would still be over a mile underwater.

Fact 644: In New Mexico, the Carlsbad Caverns have one of the world's largest underground chambers, called the Big Room. It's big enough to fit 14 football fields!

Fact 645: The city of Petra in Jordan was carved into the side of a rock cliff. You enter through a narrow gorge called the Siq.

Fact 646: Underground coal fires can burn for decades, like the one in Centralia, Pennsylvania, which has been burning since 1962.

Fact 647: In Vietnam, the Hang Son Doong cave is so large that it has its own jungle and river inside. A skyscraper could fit within its walls!

Fact 648: Sinkholes are created when the ground collapses. They can be as small as a puddle or as large as an entire city block.

CHAPTER 28:
Feats of Engineering

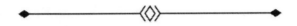

F act 649: The Great Pyramid of Giza was the tallest man-made structure for over 3,800 years. It was built without modern machinery and aligns perfectly with the points of the compass.

Fact 650: The Eiffel Tower in Paris was supposed to be a temporary structure, but it's still standing after more than 130 years and has become a symbol of France.

Fact 651: The International Space Station is the largest human-made object ever to fly in space, and it travels at a speed of 17,500 miles per hour!

Fact 652: The Panama Canal uses a system of locks to lift ships up and down so they can cross from the Atlantic Ocean to the Pacific Ocean without having to go around South America.

Fact 653: Hoover Dam in the United States was built during the Great Depression and created one of the largest man-made lakes, Lake Mead.

Fact 654: The Golden Gate Bridge in San Francisco was once the longest suspension bridge span in the world and is painted an "International Orange" color for visibility in fog.

Fact 655: The tallest building in the world, as of my last update, is the Burj Khalifa in Dubai, standing at 828 meters (2,717 feet) tall.

Fact 656: Ancient Romans built the Colosseum, which could seat around 50,000 spectators for events like gladiator battles and it even featured retractable awnings.

Fact 657: The Channel Tunnel, also known as the Chunnel, connects the UK and France. Workers from both countries met in the middle as they dug from each side.

Fact 658: The Great Wall of China is so long it stretches over 13,000 miles and some parts are over 2,300 years old.

Fact 659: The Leaning Tower of Pisa leans because its foundation was built on soft ground. It took nearly 200 years to complete because of its unstable foundation.

Fact 660: The world's longest sea bridge, the Hong Kong-Zhuhai-Macau Bridge, spans 34 miles and includes an underwater tunnel.

Fact 661: The tallest statue in the world, the Statue of Unity in India, stands 182 meters (597 feet) tall, almost twice the height of the Statue of Liberty.

Fact 662: The ancient city of Petra, carved into red desert cliffs in Jordan, was built over 2,000 years ago and includes a theater that could seat 3,000 people.

Fact 663: The Akashi Kaikyō Bridge in Japan has the longest central span of any suspension bridge in the world, at 1,991 meters (6,532 feet).

Fact 664: The Hubble Space Telescope, while not a building, is an incredible piece of engineering that orbits Earth and has taken some of the most detailed images of outer space.

Fact 665: The Bailong Elevator in China is the highest outdoor elevator in the world, made mostly of glass, and takes visitors up a cliff face.

Fact 666: The ancient Inca site of Machu Picchu in Peru was built without the use of wheels, iron tools, or even mortar to hold the stones together.

Fact 667: The Palm Islands of Dubai are the largest artificial islands in the world and required over 94 million cubic meters of sand to build.

Fact 668: The Leshan Giant Buddha in China is a 71-meter (233 feet) tall stone statue carved out of a cliff face and is over 1,300 years old.

Fact 669: The Sydney Opera House features a series of large precast concrete "shells" and is one of the most famous performing arts centers in the world.

Fact 670: The Kansai International Airport in Japan is built on an artificial island and was specifically designed to withstand earthquakes and typhoons.

Fact 671: The London sewerage system, engineered by Joseph Bazalgette in the 1860s, was a major feat of Victorian engineering and is still in use today.

Fact 672: The Millau Viaduct in France is the tallest bridge in the world, with one mast's summit at 343 meters (1,125 feet) above the base of the structure.

CHAPTER 29:
Oceanic Adventures

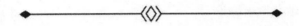

Fact 673: The Mariana Trench is the deepest part of the ocean. It's so deep that if Mount Everest were placed at the bottom, it would still be over a mile underwater.

Fact 674: The first successful trip to the bottom of the Mariana Trench was by Jacques Piccard and Don Walsh in 1960 in a submersible called the Trieste.

Fact 675: The ocean is home to the world's largest living structure, the Great Barrier Reef, which is so big it can be seen from space.

Fact 676: Viperfish, one of the creepiest looking fish in the deep sea, can use bioluminescence to attract its prey in the dark waters.

Fact 677: More than 80% of the ocean is unexplored and unmapped, which means there are probably millions of species we haven't discovered yet.

Fact 678: Underwater volcanoes, or hydrothermal vents, can shoot out water that's hot enough to melt lead.

Fact 679: The ocean has huge underwater waterfalls, like the Denmark Strait cataract, which carries 175 million cubic feet of water per second.

Fact 680: The HMS Challenger, a British ship, undertook the first global marine research expedition from 1872 to 1876, discovering over 4,000 new species.

Fact 681: The Blue Whale, the largest animal ever known to have existed, can have a heart the size of a small car.

Fact 682: Coelacanths were thought to have gone extinct with the dinosaurs until a live one was caught in 1938.

Fact 683: The ocean's biggest wave recorded was over 100 feet high, off the coast of Alaska in the North Pacific during a storm in 1958.

Fact 684: The Titanic, which sank in 1912, was not discovered on the ocean floor until 73 years later, in 1985.

Fact 685: Some species of deep-sea jellyfish can glow in the dark. This bioluminescence can scare predators or attract mates.

Fact 686: The pressure at the deepest point of the ocean is more than 8 tons per square inch, which is like having 50 jumbo jets piled on top of you!

Fact 687: Green sea turtles can migrate more than 1,400 miles to lay their eggs on the same beach where they were born.

Fact 688: The Portuguese man o' war is not a jellyfish but a siphonophore, which is actually a colony of organisms working together.

Fact 689: The deepest fish ever recorded was found at a depth of 26,722 feet in the Mariana Trench.

Fact 690: The giant squid has the largest eyes in the animal kingdom—about the size of a dinner plate—which helps it see in the deep sea.

Fact 691: In 1964, the Alvin submersible was launched, which can carry researchers to a depth of 14,800 feet for up to 10 hours.

Fact 692: Coral atolls are formed from coral reefs that grow around the edges of islands, which then sink or erode away, leaving a ring-shaped reef.

Fact 693: The Immortal Jellyfish can revert back to its juvenile form after becoming mature, potentially giving it the ability to live forever.

Fact 694: The ocean current system is often called the "Global Conveyor Belt" and moves water all around the globe, taking a full circuit about 1,000 years to complete.

Fact 695: The Gulf Stream, a warm Atlantic ocean current, is so powerful that it carries 100 times the flow of all the world's rivers combined.

Fact 696: The Mid-Ocean Ridge is the longest mountain range on Earth, stretching about 65,000 kilometers (40,390 miles), and is mostly under the ocean.

CHAPTER 30:
Mighty Rivers of the World

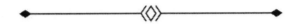

F act 697: The Nile River in Africa is the longest river in the world, stretching about 4,135 miles (6,650 kilometers). That's longer than the entire width of the United States!

Fact 698: The Amazon River in South America is so wide in places that from one bank, you can't see the other side.

Fact 699: The Yangtze River in China is the third-longest river in the world and the longest to flow entirely within one country.

Fact 700: The Mississippi River in the United States was a vital trade route for Native Americans and early European settlers.

Fact 701: The Ganges River in India is considered sacred by Hindus and is used for spiritual cleansing, despite being one of the most polluted rivers in the world.

Fact 702: The Danube River flows through 10 countries, more than any other river in the world.

Fact 703: The Volga River is the longest river in Europe, and it's so big that it accounts for about 80% of the total river flow in the European part of Russia.

Fact 704: The Colorado River carved out the Grand Canyon over millions of years; the canyon is over a mile deep in places.

Fact 705: The Congo River in Africa is the world's deepest river with measured depths in excess of 720 feet (220 meters).

Fact 706: The Thames River in London has a giant barrier that can be raised to protect the city from flooding during high tides and storm surges.

Fact 707: The Murray-Darling river system in Australia is named after its two major rivers, the Murray River and the Darling River.

Fact 708: The Rhine River is one of the longest and most important rivers in Europe, flowing through six countries on its way to the North Sea.

Fact 709: The Tigris and Euphrates rivers, which flow through Turkey, Syria, and Iraq, are often referred to as the cradle of civilization.

Fact 710: The Mekong River in Southeast Asia is home to the endangered Irrawaddy dolphin, which looks more like a beluga than a typical dolphin.

Fact 711: The Rio Grande forms a natural border between the United States and Mexico for over 1,200 miles (1,931 kilometers).

Fact 712: The Po River in Italy is so important that it's often called "Italy's rice bowl" for the rich agricultural area it creates.

Fact 713: The Hudson River was named after Henry Hudson, an English sea explorer and navigator in the early 17th century.

Fact 714: The Orinoco River in Venezuela and Colombia is one of the longest rivers in South America and is surrounded by rich, diverse rainforests.

Fact 715: The Fraser River in British Columbia, Canada, is known for the Gold Rush of 1858, where thousands of miners flocked to the riverbanks.

Fact 716: The Zambezi River in Africa is known for Victoria Falls, one of the largest and most famous waterfalls in the world.

Fact 717: The Seine in France is known for flowing right through the heart of Paris, where you can find the famous Notre-Dame Cathedral along its banks.

Fact 718: The Brahmaputra River in Asia is one of the few rivers in the world that exhibit a tidal bore, where the incoming tide forms waves that travel up the river.

Fact 719: The Saint Lawrence River connects the Great Lakes to the Atlantic Ocean and serves as a major gateway for ships entering North America.

Fact 720: The Yellow River, also known as the Huang He, carries so much yellow silt that it actually looks yellow.

CHAPTER 31:
Spectacular Space Tech

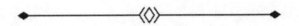

Fact 721: The Hubble Space Telescope orbits Earth and has taken some of the most detailed photos of outer space, including galaxies billions of light-years away.

Fact 722: Satellites orbiting Earth are used for all sorts of things like weather forecasting, GPS for maps, and even watching TV!

Fact 723: Mars Rovers, like Curiosity and Perseverance, are car-sized robots that explore Mars, taking pictures and samples to learn more about the Red Planet.

Fact 724: The Apollo Lunar Module, also known as the Eagle, was the first crewed vehicle to land on the Moon in 1969.

Fact 725: The International Space Station (ISS) is like a big science lab in space where astronauts from around the world live and do experiments.

Fact 726: The Voyager probes are the farthest human-made objects from Earth. They carry golden records with sounds and images of Earth, just in case they encounter alien life.

Fact 727: The Canadarm was a robotic arm used on the Space Shuttle to capture and repair satellites and build the ISS. There's also a Canadarm2 on the ISS right now!

Fact 728: Spacesuits are like personal mini-spacecraft, complete with their own air supply, cooling systems, and protection from the sun's heat.

Fact 729: The Very Large Array in New Mexico is a group of 27 huge radio antennas that work together to observe space.

Fact 730: A company named SpaceX developed the Falcon Heavy, one of the most powerful rockets ever made. It can carry satellites, supplies, and even people into space.

Fact 731: The Parker Solar Probe is a spacecraft that's flying closer to the sun than any other human-made object before it to study the sun's atmosphere.

Fact 732: The Cassini spacecraft studied Saturn and its moons for over 13 years before plunging into the planet's atmosphere in a fiery finale.

Fact 733: The James Webb Space Telescope, set to launch in the future, will be even more powerful than Hubble and will help us see the first galaxies that formed after the Big Bang.

Fact 734: The New Horizons spacecraft gave us our first close-up pictures of Pluto and its moons.

Fact 735: The Space Shuttle was the first reusable spacecraft and looked like an airplane. It flew missions for 30 years!

Fact 736: The European Space Agency's Rosetta mission successfully landed a probe on a comet, the first time in history this was achieved.

Fact 737: Spaceships use a type of engine called an ion drive which can slowly accelerate a spacecraft to very high speeds over time.

Fact 738: NASA's Artemis program aims to return humans to the Moon and establish a sustainable human presence there by the end of the decade.

Fact 739: The Kepler space telescope discovered thousands of planets outside our solar system, known as exoplanets, some of which might be similar to Earth.

Fact 740: The Juno spacecraft is studying Jupiter's atmosphere, magnetic field, and looking for clues about how the planet formed.

Fact 741: The Dragon capsule, developed by SpaceX, is one of the first commercial spacecraft designed to carry people to space.

Fact 742: Tethers Unlimited developed a technology called "SpiderFab" to 3D-print large structures in space, potentially revolutionizing how we build things in orbit.

Fact 743: The Sputnik satellite, launched by the Soviet Union in 1957, was the first artificial satellite to orbit the Earth.

Fact 744: The Cheops spacecraft is designed to study exoplanets, focusing on those where it might be possible for other forms of life to exist.

CHAPTER 32:
Animal Adaptations

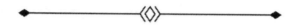

Fact 745: Camels have thick eyelashes and ear hair, plus sealable nostrils, to keep out sand in their desert homes.

Fact 746: Polar bears have black skin under their white fur to better absorb the sun's warmth and keep them toasty in icy conditions.

Fact 747: Frogs can absorb water through their skin, so they don't need to drink water like we do.

Fact 748: Some fish, like the Antarctic icefish, have a special antifreeze in their blood so they don't freeze in icy waters.

Fact 749: Giraffes have long necks to reach high leaves, but did you know their tongues are also super long to help them grab those leaves?

Fact 750: The arctic fox changes the color of its fur with the seasons—white to blend with snow in winter and brown in summer for camouflage on the tundra.

Fact 751: Kangaroos have powerful back legs that let them leap around quickly to cover large distances in the Australian Outback.

Fact 752: The dung beetle can pull over 1,000 times its body weight, making it the best weightlifter in the animal kingdom.

Fact 753: Geckos have sticky pads on their feet that let them climb up smooth surfaces and even walk upside down on ceilings.

Fact 754: The basilisk lizard can run on water for short distances, earning it the nickname "the Jesus lizard."

Fact 755: Some snakes, like the sidewinder rattlesnake, have a special way of moving that helps them slide across hot desert sand without overheating.

Fact 756: Elephants have big ears that help them cool down. They flap them like fans to shed excess heat.

Fact 757: Owls can turn their heads almost all the way around, which helps them see in all directions without moving their bodies.

Fact 758: The platypus uses its bill to detect prey underwater by sensing electric fields produced by the movements of prey.

Fact 759: Chameleons change color not just for camouflage but also to communicate with other chameleons and regulate their temperatures.

Fact 760: The bombardier beetle can shoot a hot, chemical spray from its rear end to deter predators.

Fact 761: Goats have horizontal pupils, which give them a wide field of vision to spot predators on steep, rocky terrain.

Fact 762: Octopuses can change both the color and texture of their skin to blend into their surroundings in an instant.

Fact 763: The pufferfish inflates into a spiky ball when threatened, making it difficult for predators to eat them.

Fact 764: Bats use echolocation to navigate in the dark, emitting sounds and listening for the echoes to figure out where objects are.

Fact 765: The bar-headed goose can fly at altitudes over 29,000 feet, high enough to cross the Himalayas, thanks to specialized hemoglobin in their blood.

Fact 766: The mantis shrimp has one of the most powerful punches in the animal kingdom and can break the glass in aquariums.

Fact 767: Sea cucumbers can expel their internal organs to confuse predators and then grow them back again.

Fact 768: Sloths move so slowly that algae grow on their fur, which helps camouflage them in the trees where they live.

CHAPTER 33:
Revolutions that Shaped the World

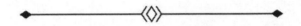

Fact 769: The American Revolution (1775-1783) led to the founding of the United States of America and introduced ideas like democracy and individual rights that many countries later adopted.

Fact 770: The French Revolution (1789-1799) ended centuries of royal rule and led to the rise of Napoleon Bonaparte. It's famous for the storming of the Bastille prison.

Fact 771: The Industrial Revolution started in Great Britain in the late 1700s and brought about machines that could do the work of many people, changing how goods were produced and how people lived.

Fact 772: The Haitian Revolution (1791-1804) was the only successful slave rebellion that led to the establishment of a free state ruled by non-whites and former captives.

Fact 773: The Scientific Revolution, which began in the 16th century, changed the way people viewed the world and led to many discoveries in physics, astronomy, biology, and chemistry.

Fact 774: The Meiji Restoration in Japan (1868) marked the end of the shogunate and restored the emperor to power, leading to rapid modernization and industrialization.

Fact 775: The Russian Revolution of 1917 ended the rule of the czars and led to the rise of the Soviet Union, the first communist state.

Fact 776: The Cultural Revolution in China (1966-1976) aimed to enforce communism by removing capitalist, traditional, and cultural elements from society.

Fact 777: The Green Revolution (1940s-1960s) greatly increased food production through new technology, crop varieties, and farming practices, helping to prevent famine in many developing countries.

Fact 778: The Iranian Revolution in 1979 replaced a westernized monarchy with an Islamic republic led by Ayatollah Khomeini.

Fact 779: The Glorious Revolution in England (1688) led to the transfer of the crown from James II to William III and Mary II without any bloodshed.

Fact 780: The Cuban Revolution led by Fidel Castro overthrew the dictator Fulgencio Batista in 1959 and established a communist government close to the United States.

Fact 781: The Digital Revolution began in the late 20th century and is ongoing. It has transformed society with the personal computer, the Internet, and the smartphone.

Fact 782: The Velvet Revolution in Czechoslovakia (1989) was a non-violent transition of power from a communist government to a parliamentary republic.

Fact 783: The Revolution of 1800 was the first time power in the United States was peacefully transferred from one political party to another after an election.

Fact 784: The Texas Revolution (1835-1836) resulted in Texas becoming independent from Mexico and later joining the United States.

Fact 785: The English Civil War (1642-1651) led to the temporary overthrow of the monarchy and the establishment of a commonwealth led by Oliver Cromwell.

Fact 786: The Color Revolutions in the early 21st century refer to various related movements that developed in several countries of the former Soviet Union and the Balkans.

Fact 787: The Young Turk Revolution in 1908 restored the constitutional monarchy in the Ottoman Empire and led to major political changes.

Fact 788: The Philippine Revolution (1896-1898) led to the first Asian republic and inspired other colonial territories to seek independence.

Fact 789: The Glorious Revolution is known for the Bill of Rights 1689, which laid out certain rights in England and later influenced the American Bill of Rights.

Fact 790: The Xinhai Revolution in 1911 ended China's last dynasty (the Qing dynasty) and led to the establishment of the Republic of China.

Fact 791: The Stonewall Riots of 1969 in New York City marked the beginning of the LGBTQ+ rights movement in the United States.

Fact 792: The Boxer Rebellion in China (1899-1901) was an uprising against foreign influence in areas such as trade, politics, religion, and technology.

CHAPTER 34:
Wilderness Survival Tales

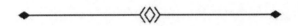

Fact 793: In 1914, explorer Ernest Shackleton's ship was trapped in Antarctic ice. He and his crew survived for months before being rescued, with Shackleton traveling 800 miles in a small boat to get help.

Fact 794: Aron Ralston, a hiker, survived a canyoneering accident in Utah in 2003 by amputating his own arm, which was trapped under a boulder, with a dull knife.

Fact 795: Yossi Ghinsberg was lost in the Amazon rainforest for three weeks in 1981. He survived with no gear and fought off wild animals before being rescued.

Fact 796: Juliane Koepcke survived a plane crash in the Peruvian rainforest when she was just 17 and trekked alone through the jungle for 11 days before being rescued.

Fact 797: In 2006, a 12-year-old girl named Akiane Kornaruk got lost in a Siberian forest for 11 days. She drank from streams and ate berries until she found her way back.

Fact 798: Douglas Mawson, an Australian Antarctic explorer, survived a solo trek over 100 miles back to base in 1913 after his two companions died.

Fact 799: Mauro Prosperi, an Italian runner, got lost in the Sahara Desert during a marathon in 1994. He survived by drinking his own urine and eating bats before finding his way to safety after nine days.

Fact 800: Joe Simpson and Simon Yates were climbing in the Andes when Joe broke his leg. Simon lowered Joe down the mountain, but Joe fell into a crevasse and had to crawl back to camp alone.

Fact 801: In 2003, teenager Ashley Merryman got lost skiing in Michigan. She dug a snow cave to survive the freezing night before being found the next day.

Fact 802: In 1952, Ann Rodgers survived nine days in the Arizona wilderness after her car ran out of gas. She lived on plants and pond water until she was rescued.

Fact 803: In 1971, LANSA Flight 508 crashed in the Peruvian jungle, and a 17-year-old girl named Juliane Koepcke survived the fall, strapped to her seat, then walked through the jungle for 10 days before finding help.

Fact 804: In 1982, Steven Callahan survived 76 days adrift in the Atlantic Ocean in a life raft. He caught fish and collected rainwater to stay alive.

Fact 805: Ricky Megee was lost in the Australian Outback for 71 days in 2006. He survived by eating leeches, insects, and frogs.

Fact 806: In 1913, Mina Benson Hubbard became the first white woman to cross the Labrador peninsula. She navigated and survived the wilderness after her husband died trying to do the same trek.

Fact 807: In 1972, a rugby team's plane crashed in the Andes. The survivors, stranded for 72 days, had to make life-or-death decisions to stay alive until rescue.

Fact 808: In 2010, 16-year-old Abby Sunderland attempted to sail solo around the world. She survived two giant waves that rolled her boat in the Indian Ocean before being rescued.

Fact 809: Ada Blackjack was the sole survivor of an ill-fated expedition to Wrangel Island in Siberia. She survived two years before being rescued in 1923.

Fact 810: In 1992, Chris McCandless ventured into the Alaskan wilderness seeking a life away from society. His survival story was made famous by the book and movie "Into the Wild."

Fact 811: In 2001, Robert Bogucki survived 43 days in the Australian Outback on minimal water and no food before being found by a television crew.

Fact 812: In 1995, Alison Hargreaves was the first woman to climb Mount Everest unaided and without supplemental oxygen. She survived harsh conditions but later died descending K2.

Fact 813: In the 1800s, Hugh Glass, a fur trapper, was left for dead after a bear attack but crawled over 200 miles to the nearest settlement, surviving on wild berries and roots.

Fact 814: In 2007, James Thompson survived a week in the Oregon wilderness after a snowmobile accident. He built a snow cave and rationed his food until he was found.

Fact 815: Nando Parrado and Roberto Canessa, survivors of the 1972 Andes flight disaster, hiked for 10 days across the mountains to find help for their fellow survivors.

Fact 816: In 1936, Joe Simpson and Simon Yates attempted to be the first to climb the West Face of Siula Grande in Peru. Joe's survival after a severe fall and the duo's separation is recounted in the book "Touching the Void."

CHAPTER 35:
World Leaders and Pioneers

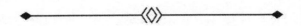

Fact 817: George Washington was the first President of the United States and is known as the "Father of His Country" for his leadership during the American Revolution.

Fact 818: Cleopatra VII was the last active ruler of Egypt and was known for her intelligence, speaking several languages, and her dramatic love life with Julius Caesar and Mark Antony.

Fact 819: Leonardo da Vinci, a Renaissance man, was not only a great artist who painted the Mona Lisa but also an inventor, scientist, and engineer.

Fact 820: Joan of Arc, a teenage girl in medieval France, claimed to hear divine voices; she led the French army to victory in several important battles during the Hundred Years' War.

Fact 821: Mahatma Gandhi was a leader in India's non-violent independence movement against British rule and is known for his philosophy of peaceful resistance.

Fact 822: Sacagawea, a Lemhi Shoshone woman, was vital to the Lewis and Clark Expedition as a guide and interpreter in the early 1800s.

Fact 823: Neil Armstrong, an astronaut, became the first person to walk on the Moon on July 20, 1969, during the Apollo 11 mission.

Fact 824: Marie Curie was a pioneering physicist and chemist who was the first woman to win a Nobel Prize and the only person to win in two different sciences.

Fact 825: Martin Luther King Jr. was a leader in the American civil rights movement and is famous for his "I Have a Dream" speech promoting racial equality.

Fact 826: Harriet Tubman escaped slavery and then helped hundreds of slaves to freedom via the Underground Railroad, and she also served as a spy during the Civil War.

Fact 827: Nelson Mandela was an anti-apartheid revolutionary in South Africa who became the country's first black president.

Fact 828: Sir Isaac Newton was a mathematician and physicist who formulated the laws of motion and universal gravitation.

Fact 829: Amelia Earhart was a pioneering aviator who was the first female pilot to fly solo across the Atlantic Ocean.

Fact 830: Alexander the Great was a king of the ancient Greek kingdom of Macedon and one of history's greatest military minds who established a vast empire.

Fact 831: Florence Nightingale was the founder of modern nursing, known for her work during the Crimean

War, where she greatly improved the conditions in war hospitals.

Fact 832: Abraham Lincoln was the 16th President of the United States and led the nation through the Civil War while working to end slavery.

Fact 833: Mother Teresa was a Roman Catholic nun who dedicated her life to helping the poor and sick in India, winning the Nobel Peace Prize for her humanitarian work.

Fact 834: Winston Churchill was the Prime Minister of the United Kingdom during World War II and is famous for his inspirational speeches and leadership.

Fact 835: Rosa Parks is known as the "mother of the civil rights movement" in America after she refused to give up her seat on a bus, sparking the Montgomery Bus Boycott.

Fact 836: Queen Elizabeth II is the longest-reigning current monarch, ascending to the throne of the United Kingdom in 1952.

Fact 837: Thomas Edison was an American inventor and businessman who developed many devices such as the phonograph, the motion picture camera, and a long-lasting electric light bulb.

Fact 838: Malala Yousafzai, a Pakistani activist for female education, is the youngest Nobel Prize laureate, known for her advocacy even after surviving an assassination attempt.

Fact 839: Julius Caesar was a Roman general and statesman who played a critical role in the events that led to the demise of the Roman Republic and the rise of the Roman Empire.

Fact 840: Frida Kahlo was a Mexican painter known for her many portraits and works inspired by the nature and artifacts of Mexico. Her work has been celebrated as emblematic of national and indigenous traditions.

CHAPTER 36:
Amazing Architecture

Fact 841: The Taj Mahal in India is a white marble mausoleum built by Emperor Shah Jahan in memory of his wife and is considered a symbol of love.

Fact 842: The Eiffel Tower in Paris was originally considered ugly by many when it was first built, but now it's one of the most recognized structures in the world.

Fact 843: The Sydney Opera House has a unique design of shell-like structures and hosts more than 1,500 performances each year.

Fact 844: The Burj Khalifa in Dubai holds the record for the tallest building in the world, reaching 828 meters (2,717 feet) high.

Fact 845: The Colosseum in Rome could hold up to 50,000 spectators in ancient times and was used for gladiator battles and other public spectacles.

Fact 846: The Great Wall of China stretches over 13,000 miles and was originally built to protect Chinese states against invasions.

Fact 847: The Leaning Tower of Pisa is famous for its unintended tilt, which started during construction due to an unstable foundation.

Fact 848: The Empire State Building in New York took only one year and 45 days to build, which was a record at that time.

Fact 849: The Lotus Temple in New Delhi, India, is shaped like a lotus flower and is a Bahá'í House of Worship that's open to people of all religions.

Fact 850: Fallingwater in Pennsylvania, designed by Frank Lloyd Wright, is famous for its design that extends over a waterfall.

Fact 851: The Petronas Towers in Kuala Lumpur, Malaysia, were once the tallest buildings in the world and are connected by a skybridge.

Fact 852: The Guggenheim Museum in Bilbao, Spain, is a modern and contemporary art museum noted for its innovative and curvy design.

Fact 853: The Forbidden City in Beijing, China, was the Chinese imperial palace for almost 500 years and consists of 980 surviving buildings.

Fact 854: The Shard in London is a 95-story skyscraper that resembles a shard of glass, hence its name.

Fact 855: The Habitat 67 in Montreal, Canada, is a unique housing complex designed for the 1967 World's Fair and looks like stacked blocks.

Fact 856: The Parthenon in Athens, Greece, was built in the 5th century BCE and dedicated to the goddess Athena Parthenos, the patron of Athens.

Fact 857: St. Basil's Cathedral in Moscow is famous for its colorful, onion-shaped domes and was commissioned by Ivan the Terrible.

Fact 858: The Chrysler Building in New York City is an Art Deco masterpiece and was briefly the world's tallest building before the Empire State Building.

Fact 859: The Space Needle in Seattle was built for the 1962 World's Fair and offers panoramic views of the surrounding area.

Fact 860: The Sagrada Família in Barcelona, Spain, is a large unfinished Roman Catholic church with an anticipated completion date of 2026, over 140 years after construction began.

Fact 861: The CN Tower in Toronto was the world's tallest free-standing structure for 32 years and is still the tallest tower in the Western Hemisphere.

Fact 862: The Louvre Pyramid in Paris serves as the main entrance to the Louvre Museum and contrasts modern architecture with the historic palace.

Fact 863: The Seattle Central Library is known for its striking modern glass and steel design, and it holds more than 1 million items.

Fact 864: The Dancing House in Prague, Czech Republic, is also known as Fred and Ginger, named after famous dancers Fred Astaire and Ginger Rogers. The building is known for its very unusual, twisting shape, which stands out among the traditional architecture of Prague.

CHAPTER 37:
The Digital Domain

Fact 865: The first electronic computer, ENIAC, was so big it filled an entire room, but it could only do basic math.

Fact 866: Email has been around since the 1970s. The first one was sent by Ray Tomlinson, and he used the "@" symbol to separate the user name from the computer name.

Fact 867: The World Wide Web was invented by Tim Berners-Lee in 1989, and he also made the first website ever.

Fact 868: Wi-Fi was invented thanks to the research of an astrophysicist, John O'Sullivan, who was looking for black holes when he helped develop a key Wi-Fi technology.

Fact 869: Emojis, used every day in texts and social media, were first created in 1999 by Shigetaka Kurita in Japan.

Fact 870: The first computer mouse was made of wood and was invented by Douglas Engelbart in 1964.

Fact 871: Google started as a research project by two PhD students, Larry Page and Sergey Brin, at Stanford University in 1996.

Fact 872: The first video ever uploaded to YouTube was called "Me at the zoo" and was only 18 seconds long.

Fact 873: CAPTCHA tests, which you sometimes have to take to prove you're not a robot on the internet, actually help digitize books by having people identify words.

Fact 874: Video games have been around since the 1950s, with the first one being a simple tennis game.

Fact 875: The first digital camera was invented in 1975 and could only take black and white photographs.

Fact 876: The term "surfing the internet" was coined by a librarian named Jean Armour Polly in 1992.

Fact 877: Bluetooth technology was named after a 10th-century king, Harald Bluetooth, who united parts of Denmark and Norway.

Fact 878: GPS (Global Positioning System) was first launched by the U.S. Department of Defense and was initially intended for military use.

Fact 879: The first smartphone was called "Simon" and was created by IBM in 1994, much earlier than the iPhone or Android phones.

Fact 880: QR codes, which can store lots of information, were created in Japan for tracking car parts in manufacturing.

Fact 881: The first animated feature film made entirely with CGI (computer-generated imagery) was "Toy Story," released in 1995.

Fact 882: Social media sites like Facebook and Twitter have changed how people communicate and get news.

Fact 883: E-books and digital libraries provide access to a wide range of books and educational materials, often for free or at a lower cost than physical books, making reading more accessible to everyone.

Fact 884: The largest data center in the world is in Langfang, China, and is almost the size of the Pentagon.

Fact 885: Minecraft, a game where you can build almost anything, is used in schools to teach kids about architecture, history, and even coding.

Fact 886: Cloud computing allows you to store your photos and documents online so you can access them from anywhere.

Fact 887: Virtual Reality (VR) headsets can transport you to different worlds, and they're not just for games; they're used for training doctors and astronauts too.

Fact 888: The first known case of a computer "bug" was in 1947 when a moth got stuck in a computer at Harvard University.

CHAPTER 38:
The Science of Sports

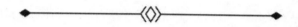

Fact 889: In baseball, the stitches on the ball create turbulence in the air, which can cause the ball to curve, known as a curveball.

Fact 890: Basketball players can seem to "hang" in the air during a jump due to the physics of projectile motion.

Fact 891: Sprinters use explosive energy stored in their muscles to dash off the starting blocks quickly. This energy comes from a compound called ATP (adenosine triphosphate).

Fact 892: In swimming, buoyancy helps keep swimmers afloat, while water resistance is what they push against to move forward.

Fact 893: Soccer balls were traditionally made from 32 panels of leather, stitched together to form a shape that's almost a perfect sphere.

Fact 894: Ice skaters glide smoothly on ice because the pressure of the skate blade causes a thin layer of the ice to melt temporarily, reducing friction.

Fact 895: When golfers hit the ball, they create backspin, which makes the ball rise higher and travel farther.

Fact 896: In gymnastics, the principle of conservation of angular momentum allows gymnasts to control their spins, flips, and turns.

Fact 897: Tennis racket strings are designed to absorb some of the impact energy from the ball, reducing stress on the players' arms.

Fact 898: Cyclists often ride closely behind one another in a technique called drafting, which reduces wind resistance and saves energy.

Fact 899: The Magnus effect explains how spin affects the trajectory of a ball in sports like tennis, soccer, and basketball.

Fact 900: In archery, the transfer of potential energy (from the drawn bow) to kinetic energy (in the arrow) is what sends the arrow flying toward the target.

Fact 901: Football helmets are designed to absorb impact energy and reduce the risk of head injuries.

Fact 902: Runners wear shoes with spikes for better traction, which helps them run faster without slipping.

Fact 903: In cricket, the seam of the ball can create unpredictable bounces and movements, challenging the batsman.

Fact 904: Skiers apply wax to their skis to reduce friction and improve glide over the snow.

Fact 905: In figure skating, skaters apply the principle of torque to pull in their arms and spin faster.

Fact 906: Bodybuilders need protein to repair and grow muscles after intensive training.

Fact 907: The dimples on a golf ball reduce air resistance and allow the ball to travel further.

Fact 908: High-altitude training is used by athletes to improve their performance because the body adapts to the lower oxygen levels by producing more red blood cells.

Fact 909: The material of a basketball shoe sole is designed to provide grip on the court and prevent sliding.

Fact 910: In baseball, the kinetic chain involves transferring energy from the legs, through the torso, and into the arms to produce powerful throws or hits.

Fact 911: Hockey pucks are frozen before games to reduce bouncing and make them slide smoothly over the ice.

Fact 912: In sports like javelin or shot put, the angle at which the object is thrown affects how far it will go, based on projectile motion physics.

CHAPTER 39:
Legendary Myths and Tales

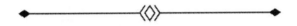

Fact 913: In Greek mythology, Hercules had to complete 12 labors, including defeating the Nemean Lion and capturing Cerberus, the three-headed dog guarding the underworld.

Fact 914: The Norse god Thor had a hammer named Mjölnir, which was so heavy that only he could lift it.

Fact 915: Anansi, a character from West African folklore, is a trickster spider who can shape-shift into a human. He often uses his wits to outsmart others.

Fact 916: In Chinese mythology, the dragon is a symbol of power and good luck and is often involved in stories about the creation of the world.

Fact 917: The legend of King Arthur from British folklore includes the famous Excalibur sword, which he pulled from a stone to prove his right to be king.

Fact 918: In Hindu mythology, Lord Hanuman is a divine monkey hero known for his strength, courage, and loyalty.

Fact 919: The Japanese tale of Momotaro, or Peach Boy, tells of a boy who emerged from a giant peach and went on to fight ogres with his animal friends.

Fact 920: In Maori mythology, Maui is a trickster hero who fished up the North Island of New Zealand using his grandmother's jawbone as a hook.

Fact 921: The Native American legend of the Thunderbird describes a powerful bird capable of creating storms and thunder with the flap of its wings.

Fact 922: In the Aboriginal Australian Dreamtime stories, the Rainbow Serpent is a major creator god and symbolizes the cycle of seasons.

Fact 923: The Greek myth of Icarus tells of a boy who flew too close to the sun with wings made of feathers and wax, which melted, causing him to fall into the sea.

Fact 924: The Norse myth of Ragnarok describes the end of the world in a great battle that results in the death of many gods.

Fact 925: According to a Filipino legend, the islands of the Philippines were created by a battle between the sky god Langit and the sea god Laut.

Fact 926: In Celtic mythology, the leprechaun is a small, mischievous fairy often associated with pots of gold at the end of rainbows.

Fact 927: The Aztec god Quetzalcoatl, depicted as a feathered serpent, was a creator god and associated with wind, air, and learning.

Fact 928: The Roman myth of Romulus and Remus tells about the founding of Rome by two brothers raised by a she-wolf.

Fact 929: In Slavic folklore, Baba Yaga is a witch-like character who flies around in a mortar, wielding a pestle, and lives in a house that stands on chicken legs.

Fact 930: The Greek goddess Athena was born from the head of Zeus, fully grown and wearing armor.

Fact 931: In Egyptian mythology, the god Anubis, with a jackal's head, was the protector of graves and guide to the afterlife.

Fact 932: The story of the Fountain of Youth, a legendary spring that supposedly restores the youth of anyone who drinks or bathes in its waters, appears in various cultures.

Fact 933: In Hindu mythology, the god Vishnu took different avatars, including Rama and Krishna, to save the world from evil.

Fact 934: The Finnish epic "Kalevala" is a compilation of folklore and mythology, telling the story of the creation of the world and the adventures of its heroes.

Fact 935: According to a legend from the Pacific Northwest, the trickster raven stole the sun from an old man to bring light to the world.

Fact 936: In Norse mythology, the World Tree, Yggdrasil, connects the nine worlds, including Asgard, home of the gods, and Midgard, home of humans.

CHAPTER 40:
The Human Impact

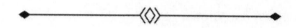

Fact 937: Humans have been around for about 300,000 years, and in that time, we've changed the planet more than any other species.

Fact 938: Agriculture, which began about 10,000 years ago, allowed humans to settle in one place and led to the growth of civilizations.

Fact 939: The Industrial Revolution in the 18th century introduced machines powered by fossil fuels, greatly increasing human impact on the environment.

Fact 940: Humans have created artificial islands by reclaiming land from the sea, like The World Islands in Dubai.

Fact 941: The invention of plastic has led to a new kind of pollution. Every year, millions of tons of plastic end up in the oceans, affecting marine life.

Fact 942: Deforestation, the clearing of forests for agriculture or urban development, has reduced habitats for many wildlife species and contributes to climate change.

Fact 943: Urbanization, or the growth of cities, has created large areas covered with concrete and asphalt, known as "urban heat islands" where temperatures can be higher than surrounding areas.

Fact 944: Air travel, a human invention, has made the world more connected but also contributes significantly to global carbon emissions.

Fact 945: The use of chemicals in farming, known as pesticides and fertilizers, has helped increase food production but also polluted waterways and harmed wildlife.

Fact 946: The extinction of many species, like the dodo bird and the passenger pigeon, was directly caused by human activities.

Fact 947: Global warming, mainly caused by burning fossil fuels, is leading to climate change, affecting weather patterns, sea levels, and ecosystems worldwide.

Fact 948: The hole in the ozone layer was caused by chemicals called CFCs used in refrigerators and aerosol sprays, but global agreements to stop using CFCs have helped the ozone layer start to recover.

Fact 949: Artificial lighting has changed how we live and work but also created light pollution, affecting both human health and wildlife.

Fact 950: Overfishing has led to the decline of many fish populations, impacting the balance of marine ecosystems.

Fact 951: The spread of invasive species, often due to human transport, has disrupted native ecosystems around the world.

Fact 952: The creation of dams for hydroelectric power and irrigation has transformed rivers, impacting freshwater habitats.

Fact 953: Plastic microbeads, used in products like toothpaste and face wash, can end up in oceans, polluting water and harming marine life.

Fact 954: Car emissions contribute to air pollution and are a major source of greenhouse gases, which drive climate change.

Fact 955: Desertification, or the spread of desert-like conditions often due to overgrazing and poor land management, is a growing environmental problem.

Fact 956: Humans have drilled deep into the Earth for oil and gas, sometimes causing environmental disasters like oil spills that harm wildlife and ecosystems.

Fact 957: Acid rain, caused by industrial emissions, damages forests, lakes, and buildings.

Fact 958: The growing demand for electronic devices has led to e-waste, which can release harmful chemicals into the environment when not properly disposed of.

Fact 959: Intensive agriculture and livestock farming contribute to the release of methane, a potent greenhouse gas.

Fact 960: Urban gardens and green spaces have been developed in many cities to bring more nature into urban areas and improve air quality.

CHAPTER 41:
Magical Mathematics

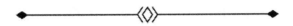

F act 961: Zero ('0') wasn't used in European mathematics until the 12th century. It was first used in ancient India.

Fact 962: A "googol" is the number 1 followed by 100 zeros. It's way bigger than the number of atoms in the universe!

Fact 963: The symbol for infinity (∞) was created by John Wallis in 1655 and it represents a value that goes on forever.

Fact 964: The most famous irrational number is Pi (π), which is the ratio of a circle's circumference to its diameter. It goes on forever without repeating!

Fact 965: In ancient Rome, numbers were written using Roman numerals. For example, the Roman numeral for 100 is 'C'.

Fact 966: The Fibonacci sequence is a series where each number is the sum of the two preceding ones, often found in nature, like in the arrangement of leaves or the pattern of a pineapple.

Fact 967: Magic squares are grids where the sum of every row, column, and diagonal are the same number. The ancient Chinese first recorded these in 650 BC.

Fact 968: The Pythagorean theorem, discovered by the Greek mathematician Pythagoras, shows that in a right triangle, the square of the longest side is equal to the sum of the squares of the other two sides.

Fact 969: The number 'five' is the only number in English that has the same number of letters as its value.

Fact 970: The word 'hundred' comes from the Old Norse term, 'hundrath', which actually meant 120, not 100.

Fact 971: In 2010, a mathematician calculated the largest known prime number, which has over 17 million digits!

Fact 972: An 'abacus' was one of the first counting tools, and it's still used in some parts of the world today to perform basic arithmetic.

Fact 973: The 'Monty Hall Problem' is a famous probability puzzle named after the host of the TV game show 'Let's Make a Deal'.

Fact 974: 'Palindrome' numbers read the same forward and backward, like 12321.

Fact 975: The ancient Babylonians had a base-60 numerical system, which is why we have 60 seconds in a minute and 60 minutes in an hour.

Fact 976: A 'perfect number' is a number that is the sum of its proper divisors. The smallest perfect number is 6 (1 + 2 + 3 = 6).

Fact 977: In geometry, a 'tesseract' is a four-dimensional analog of a cube.

Fact 978: The 'Golden Ratio' (approximately 1.618) appears in some patterns in nature, including the spiral arrangement of leaves and other plant parts.

Fact 979: 'Fractals' are complex geometric shapes that look similar at any scale and are used to model structures in nature.

Fact 980: The 'Butterfly Effect', a term in chaos theory, suggests that small changes can lead to significant effects, like a butterfly flapping its wings causing a tornado elsewhere.

Fact 981: 'Möbius strips' are surfaces with only one side and one boundary curve. If you cut a Möbius strip along the centerline, it creates one long loop.

Fact 982: 'Graham's Number' is so large that if all the digits were written out, they wouldn't fit in the observable universe.

Fact 983: The ancient Egyptians used a system of mathematics that involved multiplication by doubling, which is similar to the binary system used in modern computers.

Fact 984: A 'paradox' is a statement that contradicts itself, like the famous "This statement is false" paradox.

CHAPTER 42:
Time Travelers

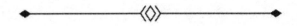

Fact 985: The Stone Age, which lasted about 3.4 million years, saw early humans use tools and weapons made of stone.

Fact 986: In Ancient Egypt, around 5,000 years ago, the pyramids were built, and they're still standing today!

Fact 987: The Roman Empire, at its peak, controlled most of Europe, North Africa, and parts of the Middle East.

Fact 988: During the Middle Ages (5th to 15th century), castles with moats were built for protection against invaders.

Fact 989: The Renaissance, starting in the 14th century in Italy, was a time of great artistic and scientific discovery, including the works of Leonardo da Vinci and Michelangelo.

Fact 990: In 1492, Christopher Columbus sailed across the Atlantic Ocean and reached the Americas, a continent unknown to Europeans at the time.

Fact 991: The Age of Exploration in the 15th and 16th centuries saw European explorers like Vasco da Gama and Ferdinand Magellan travel to new lands.

Fact 992: The Industrial Revolution began in Britain in the late 1700s, bringing machines that changed the way people worked and lived.

Fact 993: In 1776, the United States declared its independence from Britain, leading to the American Revolutionary War.

Fact 994: The Victorian Era, during the 19th century in Britain, was named after Queen Victoria and was a time of great industrial, cultural, and scientific progress.

Fact 995: The first airplane was flown by the Wright brothers in 1903, changing the way people travel.

Fact 996: World War I (1914-1918) involved many countries worldwide and led to significant changes in the political map of Europe.

Fact 997: In the 1920s, the first feature-length animated movie, "Snow White and the Seven Dwarfs," was created by Walt Disney.

Fact 998: World War II (1939-1945) saw massive global conflict and the use of nuclear weapons for the first time in history.

Fact 999: The Space Race between the United States and the Soviet Union during the Cold War led to the first man landing on the moon in 1969.

Fact 1000: The invention of the internet in the late 20th century revolutionized communication, information, and entertainment.

Fact 1001: The fall of the Berlin Wall in 1989 marked the end of the Cold War and the beginning of German reunification.

Fact 1002: The turn of the millennium in the year 2000 was celebrated around the world with fireworks and special events.

Fact 1003: In the early 21st century, smartphones changed the way people interact, access information, and entertain themselves.

Fact 1004: The COVID-19 pandemic, starting in 2019, led to global changes in health, economy, and daily life.

Fact 1005: The Ancient Greeks (around 8th century BC to 6th century AD) made significant contributions to philosophy, art, and science.

Fact 1006: The discovery of penicillin by Alexander Fleming in 1928 revolutionized medicine by introducing the age of antibiotics.

Fact 1007: The Viking Age (8th to 11th century) was marked by the Scandinavian exploration and settlement in many parts of Europe.

Fact 1008: The Inca Empire, which flourished in South America in the 15th and early 16th centuries, built an extensive road system and famous structures like Machu Picchu.

CHAPTER 43:
Future Frontiers

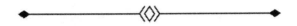

Fact 1009: Biometric technology, such as fingerprint and facial recognition, is likely to become more integrated into daily life. This technology could be used for everything from unlocking phones to personalized learning experiences in schools.

Fact 1010: Space travel could become more common, with companies like SpaceX planning to send humans to Mars in the future.

Fact 1011: Self-driving cars are being developed that can navigate and drive without human input, using sensors and advanced software.

Fact 1012: Virtual reality (VR) might become a regular part of classrooms, allowing students to take "field trips" anywhere in the world or even in space.

Fact 1013: Medical technology could advance to the point where custom organs are 3D printed for transplants, reducing waiting lists for patients.

Fact 1014: Renewable energy sources like solar and wind power might become more efficient, helping to reduce our dependence on fossil fuels.

Fact 1015: Underwater cities could be developed as a solution to overpopulation and rising sea levels due to climate change.

Fact 1016: Space hotels might become a vacation option, offering zero-gravity experiences for tourists.

Fact 1017: Wearable technology could monitor our health in real-time, alerting us to potential medical issues before they become serious.

Fact 1018: Quantum computers, much faster than current computers, might solve complex problems in seconds that would currently take years.

Fact 1019: We might establish a permanent human presence on the Moon, using it as a stepping stone for deeper space exploration.

Fact 1020: Robots could become everyday helpers, assisting with tasks ranging from household chores to complex surgeries.

Fact 1021: Hyperloop and high-speed rail systems might make travel between cities much faster than driving or flying today.

Fact 1022: Advancements in nanotechnology could lead to new materials with amazing properties, like self-healing structures or ultra-strong fabrics.

Fact 1023: Augmented reality (AR) could overlay helpful information on the real world, like showing directions or translations right in front of your eyes.

Fact 1024: Gene editing techniques like CRISPR could cure genetic diseases and potentially lead to custom-designed organisms.

Fact 1025: Personal drones might become as common as smartphones, used for everything from delivery services to personal transportation.

Fact 1026: Telescopes might become powerful enough to directly image exoplanets, giving us a closer look at potential Earth-like worlds.

Fact 1027: Smart homes could be standard, with houses that adjust temperature, lighting, and security automatically based on your preferences.

Fact 1028: Lab-grown meat, produced without raising and slaughtering animals, could become a sustainable and ethical food source.

Fact 1029: Ocean farming, not just for fish but also for plants and algae, could provide new sources of food and biofuels.

Fact 1030: Advances in AI might lead to personal assistants that understand and anticipate your needs, like a real-life version of the computer from "Star Trek."

Fact 1031: Brain-computer interfaces could allow us to control devices with our thoughts or even download our memories.

Fact 1032: Cities might become more "green" with vertical gardens on skyscrapers, urban farming, and more parks to improve air quality and biodiversity.

CHAPTER 44:
Animal Friendships

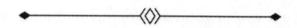

Fact 1033: A famous friendship developed between a lion, a tiger, and a bear, who were rescued together as cubs and grew up side-by-side in an animal sanctuary.

Fact 1034: Dolphins have been known to protect swimmers from sharks by swimming circles around them or directly intervening.

Fact 1035: In Australia, a wild dolphin named Fungie frequently accompanied fishermen on their trips for over 30 years.

Fact 1036: A goat and a horse at an animal rescue center became inseparable friends, with the goat even riding on the horse's back.

Fact 1037: Clownfish and sea anemones have a symbiotic relationship. The clownfish gets protection from predators, while the sea anemone gets food scraps.

Fact 1038: Capybaras, known for their gentle nature, are often seen befriending a variety of animals, including birds, monkeys, and even crocodiles.

Fact 1039: A blind horse once had a seeing-eye goat friend that helped it navigate around its pasture.

Fact 1040: In Kenya, a baby hippopotamus and a giant male Aldabra tortoise formed a bond after the hippo was rescued following a tsunami.

Fact 1041: Oxpeckers, a type of bird, have a symbiotic relationship with large mammals like hippos and giraffes by eating ticks and other parasites off their skin.

Fact 1042: A cat and an owl in Japan became playmates, with the owl often perching on the cat's head.

Fact 1043: An elephant and a sheep formed an unlikely bond at a wildlife sanctuary, with the elephant showing signs of distress when the sheep was temporarily moved.

Fact 1044: Cleaner fish help larger fish by removing parasites from their skin, benefiting both parties.

Fact 1045: A dachshund and a lion became friends at a zoo, with the dog often seen lying on top of the lion.

Fact 1046: A crow was observed bringing gifts, like shiny objects, to a young girl who regularly fed it.

Fact 1047: Tarantulas and tiny frogs live together; the frog gets protection from predators, while the tarantula's eggs are safe from ants thanks to the frog.

Fact 1048: In Japan, a koi fish and a golden retriever were seen swimming together in a pond almost every day.

Fact 1049: A farm in California had a sheep that took care of a blind cow, leading it to grazing areas every day.

Fact 1050: Remoras attach themselves to sharks and eat leftover scraps from the shark's meals, getting food and transportation.

Fact 1051: A badger and a coyote were caught on camera hunting together in California, showcasing a rare moment of cooperation between two different species.

Fact 1052: In a wildlife park, a giraffe became friends with an ostrich, and they were often seen eating and roaming together.

Fact 1053: A tiger, a bear, and a lion at a sanctuary in Georgia, USA, formed an unusual bond after being rescued from poor conditions in their youth.

Fact 1054: The mutual relationship between honeybees and flowers is essential for pollination, which helps plants reproduce.

Fact 1055: A wild boar piglet in Germany was adopted by a herd of cows and was often seen grazing and resting with them.

Fact 1056: Moray eels and cleaner shrimp work together, with the shrimp cleaning the eels' mouths and getting a meal in return.

CHAPTER 45:
Deep-Sea Discoveries

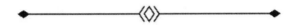

Fact 1057: The anglerfish, found in deep waters, has a glowing lure on its head to attract prey in the dark ocean depths.

Fact 1058: Giant squid live at great depths and can grow up to 43 feet long. Their eyes are as big as basketballs, the largest in the animal kingdom.

Fact 1059: The viperfish, one of the fiercest predators of the deep, has needle-like teeth so long that they don't fit inside its mouth.

Fact 1060: Bioluminescence is common in deep-sea creatures. They produce light through a chemical reaction to communicate, attract mates, or lure prey.

Fact 1061: The gulper eel can swallow prey much larger than itself, thanks to its massive, expandable mouth and stomach.

Fact 1062: The deep-sea dragonfish has transparent teeth, making them nearly invisible while hunting.

Fact 1063: Hydrothermal vents, found in deep sea, support unique ecosystems with species like giant tube worms, which can grow up to 8 feet long.

Fact 1064: The blobfish, which lives in deep waters off Australia, looks like a gelatinous blob, but its body is perfectly adapted to the high-pressure environment.

Fact 1065: The barreleye fish has a transparent head, and its eyes can look upward through its transparent dome to see prey above.

Fact 1066: The dumbo octopus, named for its ear-like fins, is one of the deepest-living octopus species, dwelling at depths of up to 13,000 feet.

Fact 1067: Yeti crabs, discovered near hydrothermal vents, have hairy arms that host bacteria, which they might use for food.

Fact 1068: The lanternfish has light-emitting organs to help it see and avoid predators in the dark ocean.

Fact 1069: Some deep-sea creatures, like certain types of jellyfish, can regenerate parts of their bodies if injured.

Fact 1070: The deep sea is home to brine pools, which are underwater lakes of super salty water that can be toxic to many marine animals.

Fact 1071: The frilled shark, a deep-sea species, has a mouth full of 300 needle-like teeth arranged in 25 rows.

Fact 1072: The cookiecutter shark, despite its small size, can take circular bites out of much larger animals with its powerful jaws and sharp teeth.

Fact 1073: The snailfish, found at depths of about 26,000 feet, is one of the deepest-living fish ever discovered.

Fact 1074: Some deep-sea animals, like certain species of sea cucumbers, can glow in the dark to ward off predators.

Fact 1075: The vampire squid, which lives in extreme depths, can turn its cape-like webbing inside out as a defensive mechanism.

Fact 1076: The megamouth shark is a rare deep-sea species known for its large head and small teeth. It was only discovered in 1976.

Fact 1077: Deep-sea creatures often have slow metabolism rates, which allow them to survive in environments with limited food sources.

Fact 1078: Black swallower fish can consume prey over twice their size and ten times their mass.

Fact 1079: The ghost shark, also known as a chimaera, has a venomous spine in front of its dorsal fin and a skull that allows it to crush prey.

Fact 1080: Some deep-sea fish have antifreeze proteins in their blood to prevent ice crystals from forming in their bodies in the cold depths.

CHAPTER 46:
Hidden Habitats

Fact 1081: Rainforests are home to more than half of the world's plant and animal species, even though they cover less than 3% of Earth's surface.

Fact 1082: Deserts aren't always hot; Antarctica is a desert because it gets very little rain or snowfall.

Fact 1083: The tundra is a cold, treeless habitat found near the North and South Poles; it's known for its permafrost, or permanently frozen ground.

Fact 1084: Coral reefs, often called the "rainforests of the sea," are some of the most diverse ecosystems on Earth.

Fact 1085: Mangrove forests are coastal habitats that have tree roots submerged in saltwater, providing homes for fish and protecting shorelines from erosion.

Fact 1086: The savanna is a grassy plain in tropical and subtropical regions, known for its large groups of animals like elephants, lions, and zebras.

Fact 1087: Wetlands are areas where water covers the soil all or part of the time, and they're important for controlling floods and providing wildlife habitat.

Fact 1088: The chaparral ecosystem, found in California and the Mediterranean, is characterized by drought-resistant plants and frequent wildfires.

Fact 1089: Cloud forests are high-altitude, moist forests that are often covered in a layer of clouds or mist.

Fact 1090: The taiga, also known as the boreal forest, is a biome characterized by coniferous forests stretching across much of Canada, Scandinavia, and Russia.

Fact 1091: The Great Barrier Reef, off the coast of Australia, is the largest living structure on the planet and can be seen from space.

Fact 1092: Grasslands, also known as prairies or steppes, are large open areas with few trees and are home to animals like bison and antelopes.

Fact 1093: The Amazon Rainforest produces about 20% of the world's oxygen.

Fact 1094: Peat bogs are a type of wetland that accumulates acidic peat, a deposit of dead plant material, often moss.

Fact 1095: Kelp forests, found in shallow oceans, are underwater areas with a high density of kelp, which are large brown algae.

Fact 1096: The Gobi Desert in Asia is the largest desert in Asia and is known for its extreme temperatures and rare snow leopards.

Fact 1097: The Atacama Desert in South America is the driest non-polar desert in the world. In some parts, it has never rained.

Fact 1098: The Serengeti in Africa is famous for its annual migration of over two million wildebeest and zebras.

Fact 1099: Paddy fields, used for growing rice, are flooded parcels of arable land, which provide the water and the conditions needed for rice cultivation.

Fact 1100: The Patagonian Desert, in South America, is the largest desert in Argentina and is known for its unique wildlife like the Patagonian mara.

Fact 1101: Estuaries, where rivers meet the sea, are full of nutrient-rich mud and are important nursery habitats for many marine species.

Fact 1102: The Himalayas, the highest mountain range in the world, have unique ecosystems and are home to animals like the snow leopard.

Fact 1103: The Mediterranean Basin has a unique type of woodland and forest habitat known for its diversity of plant life.

Fact 1104: The Dead Sea, located between Jordan and Israel, is one of the world's saltiest bodies of water, making it difficult for life to survive in it.

CHAPTER 47:
Young Inventors

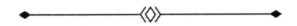

Fact 1105: Louis Braille invented Braille, the writing system used by people who are visually impaired, when he was just 15 years old.

Fact 1106: At age 12, Frank Epperson invented the Popsicle by accident when he left a mixture of powdered soda, water, and a stick in a cup outside overnight.

Fact 1107: Chester Greenwood invented earmuffs at the age of 15 to keep his ears warm during the harsh Maine winter.

Fact 1108: Philo Farnsworth sketched out the idea for the first electronic television when he was only 14 years old and later brought it to life.

Fact 1109: At 11 years old, Mikaila Ulmer founded Me & the Bees Lemonade, using her great-grandmother's recipe and adding honey to sweeten the drink, to save honeybees.

Fact 1110: Easton LaChappelle built a robotic hand out of LEGOs and fishing wire at 14, later developing it into a more advanced prosthetic limb.

Fact 1111: Gitanjali Rao, at the age of 11, invented a device to detect lead in water, inspired by the Flint water crisis.

Fact 1112: Ryan Patterson invented a glove that translates sign language into written words on a digital screen when he was a teenager.

Fact 1113: Robert Patch, at only 5 years old, created a toy truck that could be assembled and reassembled into different forms and received a patent for it.

Fact 1114: At 15, Kenneth Shinozuka invented a sensor-based device to help monitor the movement of Alzheimer's patients to prevent them from wandering.

Fact 1115: Ann Makosinski invented a flashlight powered by body heat at the age of 16, aiming to help people in developing countries without access to electricity.

Fact 1116: Alex Deans invented the iAid, a navigational device for the visually impaired, at 12 years old. It uses GPS and a compass to guide its user.

Fact 1117: William Kamkwamba built a windmill to power electrical appliances in his family's house in Malawi at the age of 14, using blueprints he found in a library book.

Fact 1118: Elif Bilgin, a Turkish teenager, developed a way to make bioplastics out of banana peels, reducing petroleum-based pollution and waste.

Fact 1119: Krysta Morlan developed the Waterbike, a device to help people with disabilities swim, at the age of 10 after experiencing difficulty swimming due to her medical condition.

Fact 1120: At 18, George Nissen invented the trampoline, inspired by trapeze artists in a circus and his own love for gymnastics.

Fact 1121: Simon Mwansa Kapwepwe, at the age of 16, invented an electronic system to control traffic lights in Zambia, aiming to reduce road accidents.

Fact 1122: Remya Jose, a teenager from India, invented a pedal-powered washing machine made from recycled bike parts to help families with no electricity.

Fact 1123: At 17, Angela Zhang created a nanoparticle that can be used to treat cancer, winning her a $100,000 scholarship.

Fact 1124: Malala Yousafzai, a Pakistani activist for female education, became the youngest Nobel Prize laureate at age 17.

Fact 1125: At age 6, Sam Houghton invented a combined broom and dustpan to help with household chores, becoming one of the youngest people ever to receive a patent.

Fact 1126: At just 14 years old, Alaina Gassler invented a system to eliminate blind spots in cars using a webcam and projector, improving driving safety.

Fact 1127: Jack Andraka invented a new method to detect pancreatic cancer at the age of 15, which is faster and cheaper than previous methods.

Fact 1128: Cassidy Goldstein solved a common problem at age 11 by inventing a crayon holder to help make broken crayons usable again.

CHAPTER 48:
Puzzle Corner

Fact 1129: The oldest known puzzle is a dissection of a square mentioned by Archimedes in 250 BC, called the Stomachion, thought to be an early form of tangrams.

Fact 1130: The Rubik's Cube, invented in 1974 by Ernő Rubik, is one of the world's best-selling puzzles. The world record for solving it is just under 4 seconds!

Fact 1131: Sudoku, a popular number puzzle, actually originated in Switzerland in the late 19th century, not in Japan.

Fact 1132: The crossword puzzle was first created in 1913 by Arthur Wynne, a journalist from Liverpool, and published in the New York World newspaper.

Fact 1133: Chess originated in India around the 6th century AD and was known as "chaturanga," which means "four divisions of the military."

Fact 1134: The game of Go, originating in China over 2,500 years ago, is one of the oldest board games still played today.

Fact 1135: Jigsaw puzzles were first created in the 1760s by a London mapmaker who mounted maps on wood and cut them into small pieces.

Fact 1136: The Magic 8 Ball, a toy used for fortune-telling or advice, was originally invented as a paperweight.

Fact 1137: The world's largest jigsaw puzzle was completed in 2011 in Vietnam, with over 550,000 pieces and measuring over 14,000 square feet.

Fact 1138: The game Monopoly was created during the Great Depression and was originally intended to teach the dangers of unchecked capitalism.

Fact 1139: Tangrams, a type of dissection puzzle from China, consist of seven flat shapes that can be put together to form various shapes and figures.

Fact 1140: The game Scrabble was invented in 1938 by an architect named Alfred Mosher Butts and was originally called "Lexiko" and then "Criss-Crosswords."

Fact 1141: In ancient Greece, Plato and other philosophers used mechanical puzzles to help teach mathematical concepts.

Fact 1142: The classic puzzle game Tetris was created in 1984 by Russian software engineer Alexey Pajitnov and was inspired by a traditional puzzle named "Pentomino."

Fact 1143: The Tower of Hanoi is a mathematical puzzle invented in 1883 by the French mathematician Édouard Lucas. It involves moving discs between pegs according to specific rules.

Fact 1144: The first known maze, the Labyrinth of Crete in Greek mythology, was said to house the Minotaur, a mythical creature.

Fact 1145: The game of checkers, also known as draughts, dates back to ancient Egypt and was found in a tomb from 1600 BCE.

Fact 1146: Leonardo da Vinci created numerous puzzles and codes, some of which are still being deciphered today.

Fact 1147: The "15 puzzle," a sliding puzzle that became a craze in the 1880s, consists of numbered square tiles in random order with one tile missing.

Fact 1148: The modern form of the jigsaw puzzle with interlocking pieces was invented by John Spilsbury, a London engraver and mapmaker, in the 1760s.

Fact 1149: The first recorded game of "Snakes and Ladders" was played in India as a moral lesson about karma and was originally called "Moksha Patam."

Fact 1150: In the 1970s, the "Pet Rock" became a popular fad. It was a smooth stone from Mexico's Rosarito Beach sold as a live pet in a custom cardboard box.

Fact 1151: The classic video game Pac-Man was invented by Toru Iwatani and was inspired by a pizza with a missing slice.

Fact 1152: The largest-ever recorded game of "Duck, Duck, Goose" had 2,135 participants and took place in Minnesota in 2010.

CHAPTER 49:
Super Science Experiments

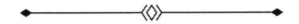

Fact 1153: Create a homemade volcano using baking soda and vinegar. The chemical reaction between the acidic vinegar and the basic baking soda produces carbon dioxide gas, causing an eruptive effect.

Fact 1154: By mixing cornstarch and water, you can make a non-Newtonian fluid called oobleck. This mixture behaves like a solid when you apply pressure and like a liquid when you let it rest.

Fact 1155: Grow your own crystals using borax, hot water, and food coloring. As the solution cools, the borax comes out of suspension and forms crystals on a string or stick.

Fact 1156: Create a tornado in a bottle by connecting two plastic bottles with water in one of them. Swirling the water in a circular motion as it flows into the second bottle demonstrates a vortex.

Fact 1157: Using a balloon and a woolen cloth, you can explore static electricity. Rub the balloon with the cloth and watch as it attracts hair or small pieces of paper due to the static charge.

Fact 1158: Plant a seed in a clear container to observe germination and root growth. This simple activity shows the early stages of plant life and the importance of water and sunlight.

Fact 1159: Make a simple electromagnet with a battery, a nail, and some copper wire. Wrapping the wire around the nail and connecting the ends to the battery creates a magnetic field.

Fact 1160: Demonstrate water density and solubility with a rainbow jar. Layer different liquids like honey, dish soap, water, and vegetable oil to see how they stack due to varying densities.

Fact 1161: Create a homemade compass using a magnetized needle, a cork, and a bowl of water. The needle, when placed on the cork and floated in water, will align with the Earth's magnetic field.

Fact 1162: Explore the power of the sun with a solar oven made from a pizza box, aluminum foil, and plastic wrap. Use the oven to melt chocolate or marshmallows, showing how sunlight can be converted into heat energy.

Fact 1163: Build a simple circuit with a battery, a lightbulb, and some wire. This introduces the basics of electrical circuits, including the flow of electric current.

Fact 1164: Investigate the science of sound by creating a homemade kazoo with a paper towel roll and wax paper. The wax paper vibrates when you hum, producing sound.

Fact 1165: Make a rain cloud in a jar using shaving cream, water, and food coloring. This illustrates how clouds hold water and how rain falls when they become too heavy.

Fact 1166: Create a simple barometer using a balloon, a jar, and a straw to learn about air pressure. As the air pressure changes, it will cause the balloon to expand or contract, moving the straw.

Fact 1167: Explore the concept of surface tension with a pepper and soap experiment. Sprinkle pepper on water, and then touch it with a soap-dipped toothpick to see how the pepper races to the edges.

Fact 1168: Build a simple hovercraft with a CD, a bottle cap, and a balloon to demonstrate air pressure and friction. The air cushion created by the balloon reduces friction, allowing the CD to glide smoothly.

Fact 1169: Make invisible ink with lemon juice. Writing with lemon juice on paper and then heating the paper reveals the secret message, showing an acid-base chemical reaction.

Fact 1170: Observe capillary action with a color-changing flower experiment. Place white flowers in colored water and watch as the petals change color due to the water traveling up the stem.

Fact 1171: Create a homemade lava lamp with oil, water, food coloring, and effervescent tablets. The reaction between the tablet and the water creates bubbles that move through the oil.

Fact 1172: Learn about chromatography with a black marker and coffee filter. The different pigments in the marker ink separate as they travel up the wet coffee filter.

Fact 1173: Use a magnifying glass and the sun to demonstrate solar energy. Focusing sunlight on a piece of paper can create enough heat to burn the paper.

Fact 1174: Make a simple pendulum with string and a weight to learn about gravity and motion. Observing the pendulum's swing shows the principles of kinetic and potential energy.

Fact 1175: Study the phases of the moon with Oreo cookies. By scraping off the cream filling to mimic the moon's phases, kids can visually and tastily learn about the lunar cycle.

Fact 1176: Create a balloon rocket to learn about propulsion and Newton's third law of motion. Stretching a balloon along a string and letting it go demonstrates action and reaction forces.

CHAPTER 50:
Coding and Computers

Fact 1177: A computer is a machine that follows a set of instructions called a program. Computers use a language called binary code, made up of ones (1) and zeros (0), to process and store information.

Fact 1178: Coding is like giving a computer a set of instructions to do something. You can create games, apps, or websites by writing code in different programming languages like Python, Java, or Scratch.

Fact 1179: The CPU, or Central Processing Unit, is the brain of a computer. It processes instructions from programs and makes the computer work.

Fact 1180: RAM (Random Access Memory) is where a computer keeps data it needs to access quickly. The more RAM a computer has, the more tasks it can handle at once without slowing down.

Fact 1181: A computer program is a list of instructions that tell the computer what to do. These instructions are written by coders or programmers.

Fact 1182: The first computer was called the ENIAC and was as big as a large room. Today's computers are much more powerful and can fit on your lap or even in your pocket.

Fact 1183: An algorithm is a step-by-step procedure to solve a problem or perform a task. Computer programs are made up of algorithms.

Fact 1184: In coding, a bug is a mistake or error in a program. Debugging is the process of finding and fixing these bugs.

Fact 1185: A computer's hard drive is where data is stored long-term, even when the computer is turned off. Things like documents, photos, and programs are stored here.

Fact 1186: The Internet is a global network of computers connected to each other. It lets computers share information and communicate.

Fact 1187: Websites are created using HTML (HyperText Markup Language), CSS (Cascading Style Sheets), and often JavaScript. HTML structures the content, CSS styles it, and JavaScript adds interactivity.

Fact 1188: A loop in coding is a way to repeat a set of instructions. For example, a loop can be used to count from 1 to 10 or to keep a game running.

Fact 1189: An operating system (OS) is software that manages a computer's hardware and software resources. Examples include Windows, macOS, and Linux.

Fact 1190: A conditional statement in programming is like a decision. It allows the program to choose different actions based on certain conditions, like "if" something is true, then do "this."

Fact 1191: A computer's motherboard is like its backbone, connecting all the different parts like the CPU, RAM, and hard drive.

Fact 1192: Wi-Fi allows computers to connect to the Internet wirelessly. It uses radio waves to send and receive data.

Fact 1193: Cloud computing means storing and accessing data and programs over the Internet instead of on your computer's hard drive.

Fact 1194: Computer viruses are harmful programs designed to damage or disrupt systems. They can spread from one computer to another, much like a cold virus spreads between people.

Fact 1195: An input device is something you use to give data to a computer, like a keyboard or a mouse. An output device, like a monitor or printer, shows or uses the data from the computer.

Fact 1196: A pixel is a tiny dot that makes up the images on a computer screen. Lots of pixels together create pictures and videos.

Fact 1197: A file format describes how data is stored in a file. Common formats include .doc for documents, .jpg for images, and .mp3 for music.

Fact 1198: A robot is a machine that can be programmed to perform tasks. Some robots are used in factories, while others can explore places like Mars.

Fact 1199: An app, short for application, is a type of software that lets you perform specific tasks. Apps can run on computers or mobile devices like smartphones.

Fact 1200: HTML tags are used to create elements like headings, paragraphs, and links on a web page. Each tag tells the browser how to display the content.

Fact 1201: In computer programming, a function is like a mini-program or a set of instructions that can be used repeatedly throughout a larger program. Functions help make code more organized, efficient, and easier to debug by allowing coders to reuse code instead of writing the same code over and over again.

Made in United States
Orlando, FL
28 November 2024

54594680R00089